MW00712048

INTERNETWORKING LANs AND WANs
Concepts, Techniques and Methods

Internetworking is one of the fastest growing markets in the field of computer communications. However, the interconnection of LANs and WANs tends to cause significant technological and administrative difficulties. This book provides valuable guidance, enabling the reader to avoid the pitfalls and achieve successful connection.

1993   0 471 93568 9

THE MULTIPLEXER REFERENCE MANUAL

Designed to provide the reader with a detailed insight into the operation, utilization and networking of six distinct types of multiplexers, this book will appeal to practising electrical, electronic and communications engineers, students in electronics, network analysts and designers.

1993   0 471 93484 4

PRACTICAL NETWORK DESIGN TECHNIQUES

Many network design problems are addressed and solved in this informative volume. Gil Held confronts a range of issues including through-put problems, line facilities, economic trade-offs and multiplexers. Readers are also shown how to determine the number of ports, dial-in lines and channels to install on communications equipment in order to provide a defined level of service.

1991   0 471 93007 5 (Book)
**   0 471 92942 5 (Disk)**
**   0 471 92938 7 (Set)**

NETWORK MANAGEMENT
Techniques, Tools and Systems

Techniques, tools and systems form the basis of network management. Exploring and evaluating these three key areas, this book shows the reader how to operate an effective network.

1992   0 471 92781 3

Please refer to the inside back cover for further details

LOCAL AREA
NETWORK
PERFORMANCE

Issues and Answers

LOCAL AREA

NETWORK

PERFORMANCE

Issues and Answers

Gilbert Held

4-Degree Consulting
Macon, Georgia, USA

JOHN WILEY & SONS

Chichester · New York · Brisbane · Toronto · Singapore

Copyright © 1994 by John Wiley & Sons Ltd.
Baffins Lane, Chichester
West Sussex PO19 1UD, England
National   Chichester (0243) 779777
International   +44 243 779777

Other Wiley Editorial Offices

John Wiley & Sons, Inc., 605 Third Avenue,
New York, NY 10158-0012, USA

Jacaranda Wiley Ltd, 33 Park Road, Milton,
Queensland 4064, Australia

John Wiley & Sons (Canada) Ltd, 22 Worcester Road,
Rexdale, Ontario M9W 1L1, Canada

John Wiley & Sons (SEA) Pte Ltd, 37 Jalan Pemimpin #05-04,
Block B, Union Industrial Building, Singapore 2057

Library of Congress Cataloging-in-Publication Data

Held, Gilbert, 1943–
    LAN performance : issues and answers / Gilbert Held.
        p.   cm.
    Includes index.
    ISBN 0 471 94223 5
    1. Local area networks (Computer networks)—Evaluation.
I. Title.
TK5105.5.H4427   1994
004.6'8—dc20
                                        93–43468
                                          CIP

British Library Cataloguing in Publication Data

A catalogue record for this book is available from the British Library

ISBN 0 471 94223 5

Typeset in $10\frac{1}{2}/12\frac{1}{2}$pt Bookman from author's disks by Text Processing
Department, John Wiley & Sons Ltd, Chichester
Printed and bound in Great Britain by Bookcraft (Bath) Ltd

CONTENTS

PREFACE

Within many organizations, LAN performance is discussed as frequently as the weather. However, unlike the weather, we have the ability to control and improve the performance of local area networks.

As I began to write this book, I returned to my original outline several times to think about the issues I face as a network manager. I am responsible for establishing new LANs and expanding existing networks. I also need to provide the communications capability for users on different networks to communicate with one another or access a number of mainframe applications which reside on different computers. Naturally, I have a fixed budget. I therefore need to determine an optimum line rate to interconnect separate networks and I must decide whether to use multiport devices or dual devices for reliability. I need to estimate network traffic for networks we plan to install but for which no prior traffic estimate exists, and evaluate the effect upon the performance of Ethernet and Token-Ring networks as those network configurations change.

These and other issues represent a core set of questions you will want to answer to ensure that your networks not only meet the requirements of your user community but in addition are not overconfigured. You will never hear an end-user complain that network performance is too good. Therefore it is likely that you will never be told that you have over-configured your network or transmission facilities. However, doing so can result in considerable over-expenditure.

In presenting various LAN performance issues, I have attempted to provide you with the tools to answer your specific networking requirements. To accomplish this goal, mathematical models of different LAN performance issues are developed. You can use these models to determine answers to your own networking requirements. Since the execution of some models is tedious and time consuming, I have included several QBASIC programs you can use to facilitate your computations.

Since a book must be finite in length, so there may well be some issues which I have overlooked or, due to space constraints, have not covered. If there is a particular issue you would like me to work upon, please feel free to contact me and I will do my best to answer your questions. Perhaps your questions, as well as the answers to those questions, will result in their inclusion in a second edition of this book. As a professional author, I value your comments and encourage you to write to me directly or through my publisher.

Gilbert Held
Macon, GA

ACKNOWLEDGEMENTS

In several books I have alluded to the fact that the development of a book is a team effort, and this book is certainly no exception.

As the author, I am directly responsible for the contents of this book; however, the many processes involved from its acquisition through its production require the skills and efforts of many individuals. Thus, I would be remiss if I did not take the time to acknowledge those individuals who certainly contributed to the development and production of this book.

As an old-fashioned writer, I like to work with pen and paper and use my notebook computer for those really labor-intensive operations, such as developing programs whose execution saves hours or days of hand-held calculator effort. In addition, the use of pen and paper provides me with the ability to easily modify drawings, which is especially convenient when you encounter turbulence at 30 000 feet or when your notebook battery low warning light illuminates. While it is easy for me to use pen and paper to develop a manuscript, it truly takes a special talent to turn that draft manuscript into a professional manuscript complete with camera-ready illustrations. Once again, I am indebted to Mrs Carol Ferrell for her fine effort in preparing the manuscript for submission.

Once a manuscript is submitted for production, a burden is removed from the author and placed upon another individual, the production manager. Responsible for numerous items which somehow all get done, Mr Stuart Gale and his team of professionals are again thanked by this author.

Last but certainly not least, the time spent writing a book places a considerable burden upon family life. Thus, my family's cooperation and understanding during the many evenings and weekends in which I worked on this book are truly appreciated.

1

LAN PERFORMANCE ISSUES

In this introductory chapter we will focus our attention upon a core set of local area network performance issues. In doing so we will discuss why such issues are important for inter- and intra-network communications in the form of questions which we will want to answer when planning or expanding a network. Although we will leave it to future chapters in this book to answer questions raised in this chapter, our discussion of performance issues serves a dual purpose. First, it makes us aware of many factors which affect the performance of individual networking devices as well as the networks to which they are connected. Secondly, it makes us aware of the fact that performance can involve the tradeoff of many operating characteristics and that in some instances the modification of the operating characteristics of a networking device to enhance its performance may require adjustments to other features of that device and other networking devices and transmission facilities. Thus, we will note that local area network performance issues in many instances involve a detailed relationship between different network components as well as the transmission facilities used to provide a connection between separate networks.

1.1 NETWORK BASICS

Readers of this book are presumed to have a degree of familiarity with the basic operation and utilization of Ethernet and Token-Ring networks. Thus, this book was not written as an introductory text on local area networks nor on local area networking concepts. However, since Ethernet and Token-Ring network performance requires a degree of knowledge concerning the format of the frames and their composition, Chapter 2 in this book reviews both areas by borrowing relevant material from the author's previous books *Token-Ring Networks* and *Ethernet Networks*, both published by John Wiley & Sons. In fact, you are encouraged to read the book most appropriate to the type of local area network you currently use or anticipate acquiring or to read both books if you intend to establish or use mixed local area networks. Doing so will provide you with a greater appreciation for network performance issues.

Each of the previously mentioned books is focused upon a specific type of local area network and provides a detailed examination of data flow on each network, the access protocol and network topology, the use of different network components, and the operation and utilization of bridges, routers, and gateways. By first reading those books you will obtain a better appreciation for the performance issues raised in the present book if your knowledge concerning the operation of either or both of those local area networks is not as detailed as you would like.

In the remainder of this chapter we will review the material in succeeding chapters with respect to the performance issues they raise. Thus, Sections 1.2 through 1.8 in this chapter can be considered previews to Chapters 2 through 8.

1.2 ETHERNET AND TOKEN-RING FRAME OPERATIONS

As previously discussed, material in Chapter 2 was first used in the author's books on Ethernet and Token-Ring networks. The key to understanding many performance-related issues is detailed knowledge of the frame format used on different local area networks—material which is presented in Chapter 2.

In Chapter 2 we will focus our attention upon the fields of Ethernet and Token-Ring frames. This will provide us with information necessary to understand the relationship between the overhead of a frame and the length of its information field. Doing so will assist us in understanding the effect of the frame length upon the efficiency of transmission on different types of local area networks. Thus, the primary focus of Chapter 2 is to provide readers with information that can be used in later chapters to answer such questions as what techniques can be used to adjust the length of local area network frames or their information transfer capability that can result in an improvement in the efficiency of transmission over the network. Other questions we will tackle in later chapters which are related to the material presented in Chapter 2 include how to determine the effect of the frame length upon bridge and router operations as well as upon their buffer memory requirements.

1.3 ESTIMATING NETWORK TRAFFIC

If we already have a network in existence, there are a large number of tools we can use to determine network traffic. Once this is done we can use the results obtained from traffic monitoring to predict the effect of a network expansion, or use such information to estimate the traffic on a similar type network which is anticipated to be established. However, what can you do to estimate traffic if your organization plans to install its first local area network or a network in which the user community will significantly differ from the users of an existing corporate network? When those situations occur you have no baseline from which you can project network traffic— a situation which can result to a significant degree in a trial-and-error approach to networking unless you have a reasonable mechanism to follow to estimate network traffic.

In Chapter 3 we will turn our attention to methods you can use to estimate inter- and intra-network traffic. After discussing the need for developing a realistic traffic measurement technique, this chapter focuses its attention upon the use of a traffic estimation worksheet which can facilitate the network traffic estimation process. This is followed by an example of the use of the worksheet to estimate the traffic load that will be placed upon a network. In addition, this chapter examines how you can use the results obtained from the use of a traffic estimation worksheet to predict future network traffic growth as well as how to analyze the potential effect of such growth upon your existing or planned local area network. Once the traffic estimation process is reviewed it is used to illustrate how you can use this data to subdivide a network via the use of a local bridge to improve network performance. Thus, this chapter provides you with information concerning the traffic estimation process, as well as illustrating its use to improve the performance level of a network.

1.4 THE IMPACT OF REMOTE BRIDGES AND ROUTERS

What is the effect upon internet transmission when data flow must cross a pair of remote bridges or routers? The answer to this question can be quite complex and is based upon the use of waiting line analysis which is an alternative term to the more popular expression known as queuing theory.

In Chapter 4 we investigate the use of waiting line analysis to network traffic which must use remote bridges or routers to reach its destination. After reviewing some of the terms associated with queuing theory we will apply it to answering some key questions associated with the use of remote bridges and routers. Those questions include 'What is an optimum line operating rate for those devices, what is the effect of using single or multiple port devices, and what is the effect of altering the memory capacity of a bridge or router upon its servicing capacity?'.

Commencing in Chapter 4 we will begin to use a series of programs developed using Microsoft Corporation's QuickBASIC compiler to facilitate performing a series of repetitive and tedious computations. The selection of QuickBASIC was based upon the fact that it is very similar to QBasic which was included in MS-DOS version 5.0 and later versions of that operating system. In addition, readers with earlier versions of DOS can easily modify the QuickBASIC programs presented in this book to operate with the BASICA or GW-BASIC interpreters included on the DOS diskette. Thus, most readers should be able to use the programs presented in this book without additional cost.

To facilitate the use of the programs contained in this book the convenience diskette contains two versions of each program. One version, contained on a file with the extension .BAS, contains the source version of the program. If you have a QuickBASIC or QBasic compiler, you can easily modify these programs to reflect your specific networking environment and then compile and execute the modified program. With a little additional effort you can also use a BASICA or GW-BASIC interpreter to execute the programs presented in this book. For those readers who desire to execute programs without modification, a directly executable version of each program is also contained on the convenience diskette. These programs have the same filename as the source language versions of the programs presented in this book but have the extension .EXE. While you cannot modify these directly executable programs, many of them operate based upon a variable input which allows you to adjust their use to your particular networking environment.

1.5 DETERMINING AVAILABILITY LEVELS

Depending upon the activities performed by your organization, you may be required to incorporate a degree of redundancy into your internet structure. To do so you can simply acquire additional pairs of remote bridges or routers and connect them through the use of separate transmission facilities. As an alternative to duplicating certain network components you can also consider the use of multiport bridges and routers whose cost is considerably less than separate devices. However, what is the difference in the level of availability provided by the use of dual port devices compared with the use of separate devices? The answer to this question as well as a detailed examination of the concept of availability, is the focus of Chapter 5.

In Chapter 5 the use of mean time before failure (MTBF) and mean time to repair (MTTR) information—usually available from vendor product specification sheets—is used to determine both component and system availability levels. Concerning the latter, a portion of this chapter illustrates how the availability level of a complex internet can be reduced to a series of simple computations.

Chapter 5 includes the use of a BASIC language program which can be used to facilitate tedious computations and provides you with the ability to compute the availability level of devices and transmission facilities connected in series or in parallel. This program also serves as a mechanism to compute the availability level of a mixed topology network. Using this program, or the calculation method described in Chapter 5, you can evaluate the costs and benefits in terms of network availability of alternative internet configurations.

1.6 ETHERNET NETWORK PERFORMANCE

Just how fast can frames flow on an Ethernet network? While this question may appear to be taken from a technically oriented game show, in actuality the answer has a considerable bearing on the performance level of bridges and routers prior to those devices becoming possible network bottlenecks.

In Chapter 6 we turn our attention to the carrier sense multiple access with collision detection (CSMA/CD) network access protocol. By closely examining this protocol we can determine the maximum frame rate that can be supported on a 10-Mbps Ethernet network based upon different frame lengths. This in turn provides us with the ability to determine if the performance level of a bridge or router listed by a manufacturer is an appropriate decision criterion for equipment acquisition. That is, if the performance level of a device is over a certain frame forwarding rate which represents the maximum frame rate that can be supported on an Ethernet network, the ability of a bridge or router to transfer frames beyond that rate is superfluous if the device supports only one communications circuit. Thus, the ability of one vendor's bridge or router to forward frames at a faster rate than another vendor's product might not be relevant when evaluating competitive products.

Once the Ethernet frame rate is determined, Chapter 6 then presents you with an easy-to-use method to predict throughput between interconnected networks. This method permits you to estimate the best-case transfer time to upload or download files across connected networks as well as to project the average time required to perform those activities.

1.7 TOKEN-RING NETWORK PERFORMANCE

The question previously asked concerning how fast frames can flow on Ethernet networks is also applicable to Token-Ring networks. That is, if you can determine the flow of information on a Token-Ring network you can use this information to estimate the performance of the network as additional stations are added to the network. You can also use this information to determine the filtering and forwarding rates required by bridges and routers connected to a Token-Ring network prior to those devices potentially becoming a bottleneck and congesting the flow of data between networks. Last but not least, by determining the frame flow on a Token-Ring network you can use this information to develop a model to project internet transmission time. If the internet is to be created or was created through the use of a wide area network transmission facility, you can easily adjust the model to reflect different WAN operating rates. Then, you can determine an optimum wide area network operating rate that will satisfy your organization's internet communications requirements without having to simply guess upon the selection of a WAN transmission facility or initiate an expensive trial-and-error process.

As might be expected from the first paragraph in this section, the initial focus of Chapter 7 is upon the development of a model to reflect the flow of frames on a Token-Ring network. Once this is accomplished the model will be exercised to determine the frame carrying capacity of a Token-Ring network under different operating conditions and network configurations.

The development of a Token-Ring traffic model will require the consideration of a large number of operating conditions and network configuration data. Some of the parameters that will have a bearing upon the flow of frames on a Token-Ring network include the number of stations on the network, the length of each lobe and the length of the ring, the average frame size, and the operating rate of the network. To facilitate our computations, we will again turn to the BASIC programming language and develop several programs to facilitate our computations. Both the Token-Ring program listings and results from executing each program are contained in this chapter. In addition, readers are referred to a set of tables contained in Appendix B which can be used to reduce the Token-Ring frame flow projection process to a simple table lookup operation.

Once the Token-Ring model is developed and exercised this information is used as a foundation for determining bridge and router performance requirements. In doing so, frame flow information is used to project a range of performance that network devices should support as well as the effect of network changes upon the frame flow on a Token-Ring network.

1.8 TRANSMISSION OPTIMIZATION

Network administrators and managers are always looking for methods that can increase the performance of their network. In doing so, they must examine and compare the use of equipment manufactured by different vendors and determine if the features of such equipment provide the capability to optimize the use of the bandwidth on a network or a wide area network transmission facility. However, prior to examining the capability and functionality of local area networking equipment, it is important to understand the key techniques that can be used to optimize network and internet transmission. Thus, the purpose of Chapter 8 is to answer the question 'What are some of the key techniques available that can be used to optimize network and internet transmission?'.

In Chapter 8 we will examine features of bridges and routers developed by manufacturers to enhance transmission. Such features include the ability to filter frames, subdivide a queue into different areas to prioritize traffic, truncate frames, and use the switched network to overcome short periods of congestion. Concerning the latter, the use of the switched network as a supplement to the use of leased analog or digital transmission facilities to connect remote bridges or routers during peak periods of internet activity provides you with the ability to economize upon your internet design. That is, you can use the switched network to satisfy peak transmission periods and size the operating rate of the wide area network transmission facility for average internet traffic. Doing so may provide you with the ability to economize upon the cost of establishing or maintaining internet transmission facilities while maintaining or surpassing the transmission requirements of your organization.

2

ETHERNET AND TOKEN-RING FRAME OPERATIONS

The key to understanding local area network performance issues is a detailed level of knowledge concerning the flow of data on a network. To understand how data flows on a local area network we must examine the method by which information is carried within a frame and how different frame fields are used to provide such functions as routing, error detection, and other network functions. Thus, the purpose of this chapter is to obtain a detailed understanding of the composition of Ethernet and Token-Ring frames, including their frame fields and the function of each field within a frame. This will provide us with the ability to understand the overhead associated with different network frames with respect to the field actually used to transport information, how network access occurs, network addressing considerations, and similar information that we must consider in attempting to determine problems that may occur when establishing or expanding a network or in attempting to connect two previously independent networks. In examining local area network frame operations, we will first focus our attention upon the frame format used on an Ethernet network and then examine the three types of transmission formats supported by a Token-Ring network.

2.1 ETHERNET FRAME OPERATIONS

In this section we will first look at the composition of different types of Ethernet frames. In actuality, there is only one Ethernet frame, while the CSMA/CD frame format standardized by the IEEE is technically referred to as an 802.3 frame. However, in this book we will collectively refer to CSMA/CD operations as Ethernet and when appropriate indicate differences between Ethernet and the IEEE 802.3 Ethernet-based CSMA/CD standard by a comparison of the two. One such area worthy of a comparison is the frame format which differs between Ethernet and the IEEE 802.3 Ethernet-based CSMA/CD standard. Once we obtain an understanding of the composition of Ethernet and IEEE 802.3 frames, we will examine the function of fields within each frame and then discuss the overhead of the frame with respect to its information transfer capability.

Frame composition

Figure 2.1 illustrates the general frame composition of Ethernet and IEEE 802.3 frames. In comparing the format of Ethernet and IEEE 802.3 frames, you will note that they slightly differ. An Ethernet frame contains an eight-byte preamble, while the IEEE 802.3 frame contains a seven-byte preamble followed by a one-byte start of frame delimiter field. A second difference between the composition of Ethernet and IEEE 802.3 frames concerns the two-byte Ethernet type field. That field is used by Ethernet to specify the protocol carried in the frame, enabling several protocols to be carried independently of one another. Under the

Ethernet

Preamble	Destination Address	Source Address	Type	Data	Frame Check Sequence
8 bytes	6 bytes	6 bytes	2 bytes	46-1500 bytes	4 bytes

IEEE 802.3

Preamble	Start of Frame Delimiter	Destination Address	Source Address	Length	Data	Frame Check Sequence
7 bytes	1 byte	2/6 bytes	2/6 bytes	2 bytes	46-1500 bytes	4 bytes

Figure 2.1 Ethernet and IEEE 802.3 frame formats.

IEEE 802.3 frame format, the type field was replaced by a two-byte length field which specifies the number of bytes that follow that field as data.

The differences between Ethernet and IEEE 802.3 frames, while minor, make the two incompatible with one another. This means that your network must contain either all Ethernet compatible network interface cards (NICs) or all IEEE 802.3 compatible NICs. Fortunately, the fact that the IEEE 802.3 frame format represents a standard resulted in most vendors now marketing 802.3 compliant hardware and software. Although a few vendors continue to manufacture Ethernet or dual functioning Ethernet/IEEE 802.3 hardware, such products are primarily used to provide organizations with the ability to expand previously developed networks without requiring the wholesale replacement of NICs. While the IEEE 802.3 standard has essentially replaced Ethernet due to their similarities and the fact that 802.3 was based upon Ethernet, we will consider both to be Ethernet. Now that we have an overview of the structure of Ethernet and 802.3 frames, let's probe deeper and examine the composition of each frame field. In doing so we will take advantage of the similarity between Ethernet and IEEE 802.3 frames and examine the fields of each frame on a composite basis, noting the differences between the two when appropriate.

Preamble field

The preamble field consists of eight (Ethernet) or seven (IEEE 802.3) bytes of alternating 1 and 0 bits. The purpose of this field is to announce the frame as well as enable all receivers on the network to synchronize themselves to the incoming frame. In addition, this field by itself under Ethernet or in conjunction with the start of frame delimiter field under the IEEE 802.3 standard ensures there is a minimum spacing period of 9.6 ms between frames for error detection and recovery operations.

Start of frame delimiter field

This field is only applicable to the IEEE 802.3 standard and can be viewed as a continuation of the preamble. In fact, the composition of this field continues in the same manner as the format of the preamble, with alternating 1 and 0 bits used for the first six bit positions of this one-byte field. The last two bit positions of this field are 11, which breaks the synchronization pattern and alerts the receiver that frame data follows.

Both the preamble field and the start of frame delimiter field are removed by the controller when it places a received frame in its buffer. Similarly, when a controller transmits a frame, it prefixes the frame with those two fields if it is transmitting an IEEE 802.3 frame or with a preamble field if it is transmitting a true Ethernet frame.

Destination address field

The destination address identifies the recipient of the frame. Although this may appear to be a simple field, in actuality this field can vary between IEEE 802.3 and Ethernet frames with respect to field length. In addition, each field can consist of two or more subfields whose settings govern such network operations as the type of addressing used on the LAN and whether or not the frame is addressed to a specific station or more than one station. To obtain an appreciation for the use of this field, let's examine how it is used under the IEEE 802.3 standard as one of the two field formats is applicable to Ethernet.

Figure 2.2 illustrates the composition of the source and destination address fields. As indicated, the two-byte source and destination address fields are only applicable to IEEE 802.3 networks, while the six-byte source and destination address fields are applicable to both Ethernet and IEEE 802.3 networks.

Although you can select either a two- or a six-byte destination address field, when working with IEEE 802.3 equipment, all stations on the LAN must use the same addressing structure. Today, almost all 802.3 networks use six-byte addressing since the inclusion of a two-byte field option was primarily designed to accommodate early LANs that use 16-bit address fields.

I/G subfield

The one-bit I/G subfield is set to a 0 to indicate the frame is destined to an individual station, while a setting of 1 indicates that the frame is addressed to more than one station. Here the latter situation indicates a group address.

One special example of a group address is the assignment of all 1's to the address field. Here the address, hex

A. 2 byte field (IEEE 802.3)

B. 6 byte field (Ethernet and IEEE 802.3)

I/G bit subfield   '0' = individual address   '1' = group address
U/L bit subfield   '0' = universally administrated addressing
                   '1' = locally administrated addressing

* Set to '0' in source address field

Figure 2.2   Source and destination address field formats.

FFFFFFFFFFFF, is recognized as a broadcast address and each station on the network will receive and accept frames with that destination address.

When a destination address specifies a single station, the address is referred to as a unicast address. A group address which defines multiple stations is known as a multicast address, while a group address which specifies all stations on the network is, as previously mentioned, referred to as a broadcast address.

U/L subfield

The U/L subfield is only applicable to the six-byte destination address field. The setting of this field's bit position indicates whether the destination address is an address that was assigned by the IEEE (universally administered) or assigned by the organization via software (locally administered).

Universal vs locally administered addressing

Each Ethernet Network Interface Card (NIC) contains a unique address burned into its read-only memory (ROM) at the time of manufacture. To ensure this universally administered address is not duplicated, the IEEE assigns blocks of addresses to each manufacturer. Those addresses normally include a three-byte prefix which identifies the manufacturer and is assigned by the IEEE as well as a three-byte suffix which is assigned by the adapter manufacturer to its NIC. For example, the prefix hex 02608C identifies an NIC manufactured by 3Com, while a prefix of hex 008002 identifies an NIC manufactured by Digital Equipment Corporation.

Although the use of universally administered addressing eliminates the potential for duplicate network addresses, it does not provide the flexibility obtainable from locally administered addressing. For example, under locally administered addressing, you can configure mainframe software to work with a predefined group of addresses via a gateway PC. Then, as you add new stations to your LAN you simply use your installation program to assign a locally administered address to the NIC instead of using its universally administered address. As long as your mainframe computer has a pool of locally administered addresses which includes your recent assignment, you do not have to modify your mainframe communications software configuration. Since the modification of mainframe communications software typically requires a recompile and reload activity to be performed, doing so requires the attached network to become inoperative for a short period of time. As a large mainframe may service hundreds to thousands of users, such changes are normally performed late in the evening or during a weekend, making the changes for the use of locally administered addressing more responsive to users than the changes required when universally administered addressing is used.

Source address field

The source address field identifies the station that transmitted the frame. Similar to the destination address field, the source address can be either two or six bytes in length.

The two-byte source address is supported only under the IEEE 802.3 standard and requires the use of a two-byte destination address, with all stations on the network required to be set to two-byte addressing field use. The six-byte source address field is supported by both Ethernet and the IEEE 802.3 standard. When a six-byte address is used, the first three bytes represent the address assigned by the IEEE to the manufacturer for incorporation into each NIC's ROM. The vendor then normally assigns the last three bytes to each of its NICs.

Type field

The two-byte type field applies only to the Ethernet frame. This field identifies the higher-level protocol contained in the data field. Thus, this field informs the receiving device how to interpret the data field.

Under Ethernet, multiple protocols can exist on the LAN at the same time, and Xerox served as the custodian of Ethernet address ranges licensed to NIC manufacturers as well as defining the protocols supported by the assignment of type field values. Under the IEEE 802.3 standard, the type field was replaced by a length field which precludes compatibility between pure Ethernet and 802.3 frames.

Length field

The two-byte length field applies only to the IEEE 802.3 standard and defines the number of bytes contained in the data field. Under both Ethernet and IEEE 802.3 standards, the minimum size frame must be 64 bytes in length from preamble through FCS fields. This minimum size frame was required to ensure that there was sufficient transmission time to enable Ethernet NICs to accurately detect collisions based upon the maximum Ethernet cable length specified for a network and the time required for a frame to propagate the length of the cable. The minimum frame length of 64 bytes and the possibility of using two-byte addressing fields mean that each data field must be a minimum of 46 bytes in length.

Data field

As previously discussed, the data field must be a minimum of 46 bytes in length to ensure the frame is at least 64 bytes in length. This means that the transmission of one byte of information must be carried within a 46-byte data field and results in the padding of the remainder of the field if the information to be placed in the field is less than 46 bytes in length. Although some publications subdivide the data field to include a PAD subfield, the latter actually represents optional fill characters that are added to the information in the data field to ensure a length of 46 bytes. The maximum length of the data field is 1500 bytes, which results in the use of multiple frames to transport full screen images and almost all file transfers.

Frame check sequence field

The frame check sequence (FCS) field is applicable to both Ethernet and the IEEE 802.3 standard and provides a mechanism for error detection. Each transmitter computes a cyclic redundancy check (CRC) which covers both address fields, the type/length field, and the data field. The transmitter then places the computed CRC in the four-byte FCS field.

The CRC is developed by treating the composition of the previously mentioned fields as one long binary number. The n bits to be covered by the CRC are considered to represent the coefficients of a polynomial $M(X)$ of degree $n-1$. Here, the first bit in the destination address field corresponds to the X^{n-1} term, while the last bit in the data field corresponds to the X^0 term. Next, $M(X)$ is multiplied by X^{32} and the result of that multiplication process is divided by the following polynomial:

$$G(X) = X^{32} + X^{26} + X^{23} + X^{22} + X^{16} + X^{12} + X^{11} + X^{10} + X^8 + X^7 +$$

$$X^5 + X^4 + X^3 + X + 1$$

Readers should note that the term X^n represents the setting of a bit to a 1 in position n. Thus, part of the generating polynomial $X^5 + X^4 + X^3 + X^1$ represents the binary value 110111.

The result of the division produces a quotient and remainder. The quotient is discarded and the remainder becomes the CRC value placed in the four-byte FCS field. This 32-bit CRC reduces the probability of an undetected error to 1 bit in every 4.3 billion, or approximately 1 bit in $2^{32} - 1$ bits.

Once a frame reaches its destination, the receiver uses the same polynomial to perform the same operation upon the received data. If the CRC computed by the receiver matches the CRC in the FCS field, the frame is accepted. Otherwise, the receiver discards the received frame as it is considered to have one or more bits in error. The receiver will also consider a received frame to be invalid and discard it under two additional conditions. Those conditions occur when the frame does not contain an integral number of bytes and when the length of the data field does not match the value contained in the length field. Obviously the latter condition applies only to the 802.3 standard since an Ethernet frame uses a type field instead of a length field.

Frame overhead

As previously indicated in this section, each Ethernet frame consists of six fields (if we consider the preamble and start of frame delimiter as one field), of which only one field actually transports information. That data field must contain a minimum of 46 bytes even if the frame is transporting a single character response to a client–server query. Thus, the overhead associated with an Ethernet frame depends upon both the fixed length of the frame fields that do not carry information as well as the number of characters carried in the data field, which can vary from one to 1500 bytes.

If we assume six-byte addressing which is applicable to almost all modern Ethernet networks, the number of fixed overhead bytes per frame is 26, consisting of eight preamble bytes, six destination and six source address bytes, two bytes for the type or length field, and four bytes for the FCS field.

A one-byte response carried in the data field must be padded by the addition of 37 fill characters when six-byte addressing is used. In this situation the overhead required to carry a one-byte character is 26 plus 37, or 63 bytes.

Now consider the situation in which you have 38 bytes of data to transmit. Here the 38 bytes would not require the addition of pad characters since the frame length when using six-byte addressing would be 64 bytes which is the minimum frame length. Thus, 38 bytes of data would result in a frame overhead of 26 bytes.

Table 2.1 summarizes the overhead associated with transporting information in Ethernet frames as the number of bytes of information varies from one to the maximum 1500 bytes the frame can carry. As indicated in Table 2.1, this overhead can vary considerably, ranging from a high of 6300% to a low of 1.7% when the maximum length data field is used to transport information.

Table 2.1 Ethernet frame overhead.

Information carried in data field (bytes)	Frame overhead (bytes)	Percent overhead
1	63	6300.0
38	26	68.4
39	26	66.7
64	26	40.6
128	26	20.3
256	26	10.2
512	26	5.1
1 024	26	2.5
1 500	26	1.7

One question you might have by now is how you can use the overhead information presented in Table 2.1 to your advantage for increasing network performance. The data contained in Table 2.1 can be extremely important for network performance if your organization is developing client–server applications. For example, assume your programming staff is developing screens to be displayed on a user's workstation in which the client enters information which is then transmitted to the server to initiate different activities. If there is a choice between generating a screen display which results in the transmission of a small number of characters to the server or generating a lesser number of screen displays and transmitting the fields of several screens at one time, the latter is preferable as it results in a lower overhead. This in turn will reduce the number of frames carried on the network. Since Ethernet requires a fixed time gap between frames, reducing the number of frames increases the efficiency of the data flow. While altering the transmission of data carried by frames will probably not result in any noticeable increase in network performance if your network only has a handful of workstations, more notable results can be expected to be observed if your network has a large number of stations that perform client–server operations on a regular basis.

2.2 TOKEN-RING FRAME FORMATS

Three types of frame formats are supported on a Token-Ring network—token, abort, and frame. The token format as illustrated at the top of Figure 2.3 is the mechanism by which access to the ring is passed from one computer attached to the

a. Token format

b. Abort token format

Starting delimiter	Ending delimiter

c. Frame format

Starting delimiter (8 bits)	Access control (8 bits)	Frame control (8 bits)	Destination address (48 bits)	Source address (48 bits)	Routing information (optional)

Information variable	Frame check sequence (32 bits)	Ending delimiter (8 bits)	Frame status (8 bits)

Figure 2.3 a: Token, b: abort, and c: frame formats. P = priority bits, T = token bit, M = monitor bit, R = reservation bits.

network to another device connected to the network. Here the token format consists of three bytes, of which the starting and ending delimiters are used to indicate the beginning and end of a token frame. The middle byte of a token frame is an access control byte. Three bits are used as a priority indicator, three bits are used as a reservation indicator, while one bit is used for the token bit, and another bit position functions as the monitor bit.

When the token bit is set to a binary 0 it indicates that the transmission is a token. When it is set to a binary 1 it indicates that data in the form of a frame is being transmitted.

The second Token-Ring frame format signifies an abort token. In actuality there is no token, since this format is indicated by a starting delimiter followed by an ending delimiter. The transmission of an abort token is used to abort a previous transmission. The format of an abort token is illustrated in Figure 2.3b.

The third type of Token-Ring frame format occurs when a station seizes a free token. At that time the token format is converted into a frame which includes the addition of frame control, addressing data, an error detection field and a frame status field. The format of a Token-Ring frame is illustrated in Figure 2.3c.

Frame composition

By examining each of the fields in the Token-Ring frame we can examine the token and token abort frames due to the commonality of fields between each frame. Note that excluding the optional routing field there is a total of 21 bytes of overhead associated with a Token-Ring frame.

Starting/ending delimiters

The starting and ending delimiters mark the beginning and ending of a token or frame. Each delimiter consists of a unique code pattern which identifies it to the network. To understand the composition of the starting and ending delimiter fields requires us to review the method by which data is represented on a Token-Ring network using Differential Manchester encoding.

Differential Manchester encoding

Figure 2.4 illustrates the use of Differential Manchester encoding, comparing its operation to non-return to zero (NRZ) and conventional Manchester encoding.

At the top of Figure 2.4, NRZ coding illustrates the representation of data by holding a voltage low (−V) to represent a binary 0 and high (+V) to represent a binary 1. This method of signaling is called non-return to zero since there is no return to a 0 V position after each data bit is coded.

One problem associated with NRZ encoding is the fact that a long string of 0 or 1 bits does not result in a voltage change. Thus, to determine that bit m in a string of n bits of 0's or 1's is set to a 0 or 1 requires sampling at predefined bit times. This

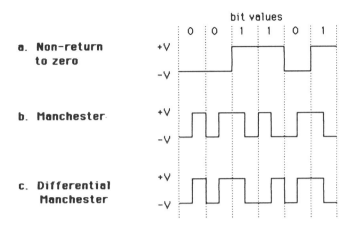

Figure 2.4 a: Non-return to zero (NRZ), b: Manchester, and c: Differential Manchester encoding. In Differential Manchester encoding, the direction of the signal's voltage transition changes whenever a binary 1 is transmitted but remains the same for a binary 0.

in turn requires each device on a network using NRZ encoding to have its own clocking circuitry.

To avoid the necessity of building clocking circuitry into devices requires a mechanism for encoded data to carry clocking information. One method by which encoded data carries clocking information is obtained from the use of Manchester encoding which is illustrated in Figure 2.4b. In Manchester encoding, each data bit consists of a half-bit time signal at a low (negative) voltage (−V) and another half-bit time signal at the opposite (positive) voltage (+V). Every binary 0 is represented by a half-bit time at a low voltage and the remaining half-bit time at a high voltage. Every binary 1 is represented by a half-bit time at a high voltage followed by a half-bit time at a low voltage. By changing the voltage for every binary digit, Manchester encoding insures that the signal carries self-clocking information.

In Figure 2.4c, Differential Manchester encoding is illustrated. The difference between Manchester encoding and Differential Manchester encoding occurs in the method by which binary 1's are encoded. In Differential Manchester encoding, the direction of the signal's voltage transition changes whenever a binary 1 is transmitted, but remains the same for a binary 0. The IEEE 802.5 standard specifies the use of Differential Manchester encoding and this encoding technique is used on Token-Ring networks at the physical layer to transmit and detect four distinct symbols — a binary 0, a binary 1, and two non-data symbols.

Non-data symbols

Under Manchester and Differential Manchester encoding there are two possible code violations that can occur. Each code violation produces what is known as a non-data symbol and is used in the Token-Ring frame to denote starting and ending delimiters similar to the use of the flag in an HDLC frame. However, unlike the flag whose bit composition, 01111110, is uniquely maintained by inserting a 0 bit after every sequence of five set bits and removing a 0 following every sequence of five set bits, Differential Manchester encoding maintains the uniqueness of frames by the use of non-data J and non-data K symbols. This eliminates the bit stuffing operations required by HDLC.

The two non-data symbols each consist of two half-bit times without a voltage change. The J symbol occurs when the voltage is the same as that of the last signal, while the K symbol occurs when the voltage becomes the opposite of that of the last signal. Figure 2.5 illustrates the occurrence of the J and K non-data symbols based upon different last-bit voltages. Readers will note in comparing Figure 2.5 to Figure 2.4c that the J and K non-data symbols are distinct code violations that cannot be mistaken for either a binary 0 or a binary 1.

Now that we have an understanding of the operation of Differential Manchester encoding and the composition of the J and K non-data symbols, we can focus our attention upon the actual format of each frame delimiter.

The start delimiter field marks the beginning of a frame.

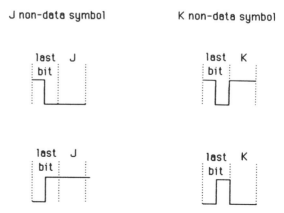

Figure 2.5 J and K non-data symbol composition. J and K non-data symbols are distant code violations that cannot be mistaken for data.

The composition of this field is the bits and non-data symbols JK0JK000. The end delimiter field marks the end of a frame as well as denoting whether or not the frame is the last frame of a multiple frame sequence using a single token or if there are additional frames following this frame. The format of the end delimiter field is JK1JK1IE, where I is the intermediate frame bit. If I is set to 0, this indicates it is the last frame transmitted by a station. If I is set to 1, this indicates that additional frames follow this frame. E is an Error-Detected bit. The E bit is initially set to 0 by the station transmitting a frame, token, or abort sequence. As the frame circulates the ring, each station checks the transmission for errors. Upon detection of a Frame Check Sequence (FCS) error, inappropriate non-data symbol, illegal framing, or another type of error, the first station detecting the error will set the E bit to a value of 1. Since stations keep track of the number of times they set the E bit to a value of 1, it becomes possible to use this information as a guide to locating possible cable errors. For example, if one workstation accounted for a very large percentage of E bit settings in a 72-station network, there is a high degree of probability that there is a problem with the lobe cable to that workstation. The problem could be a crimped cable or a loose connector and represents a logical place to commence an investigation in an attempt to reduce E bit errors.

Access control field

The second field in both token and frame formats is the access control byte. As illustrated in Figure 2.3a, this byte consists of four subfields and serves as the controlling mechanism for gaining access to the network. When a free token circulates the network the access control field represents one-third of the length of the frame since it is prefixed by the start delimiter and suffixed by the end delimiter.

The lowest priority that can be specified by the priority bits in the access control byte is zero (000), while the highest is seven (111), providing eight levels of priority. Table 2.2 lists the normal use of the priority bits in the access control field. Workstations have a default priority of three, while bridges have a default priority of four.

To reserve a token, a workstation inserts its priority level in the priority reservation subfield. Unless another station with a higher priority bumps the requesting station, the reservation

Table 2.2 Priority bit settings.

Priority bits	Priority	
000	0	Normal user priority, MAC frames that do not require a token and response type MAC frames
001	1	Normal user priority
010	2	Normal user priority
011	3	Normal user priority and MAC frames that require tokens
100	4	Bridge
101	5	Reserved
110	6	Reserved
111	7	Specialized Station Management

will be honored and the requesting station will obtain the token. If the token bit is set to 1, this serves as an indication that a frame follows instead of the ending delimiter.

A station that needs to transmit a frame at a given priority can use any available token that has a priority level equal to or less than the priority level of the frame to be transmitted. When a token of equal or lower priority is not available, the ring station can reserve a token of the required priority through the use of the reservation bits. In doing so the station must follow two rules. First, if a passing token has a higher priority reservation than the reservation level desired by the workstation, the station will not alter the reservation field contents. Secondly, if the reservation bits have not been set or indicate a lower priority than that desired by the station, the station can now set the reservation bits to the required priority level.

Once a frame is removed by its originating station, the reservation bits in the header will be checked. If those bits have a non-zero value, the station must release a non-zero priority token, with the actual priority assigned based upon the priority used by the station for the recently transmitted frame, the reservation bit settings received upon the return of the frame, and any stored priority.

Upon occasion, the Token-Ring protocol will result in the transmission of a new token by a station prior to that station having the ability to verify the settings of the access control field in a returned frame. When this situation arises, the token will be issued according to the priority and reservation bit settings in the access control field of the transmitted frame.

Figure 2.6 illustrates the operation of the priority (P) and reservation (R) bit fields in the access control field. In this example,

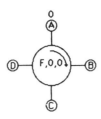

a. Station A generates a frame
using a non-priority token P,R=0,0.

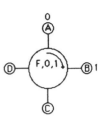

b. Station B reserves a priority
1 in the reservation bits in
the frame P,R=0,1; Station A
enters a priority-hold state.

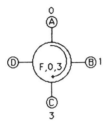

c. Station C reserves a priority of 3,
overriding B's reservation of 1; P,R=0,3.

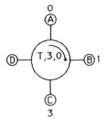

d. Station A removes its frame and
generates a token at reserved
priority level 3; P,R=3,0.

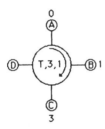

e. Station B repeats priority token and
makes a new reservation of priority
level 1; P,R=3,1

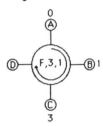

f. Station C grabs token and
transmits a frame with a priority
of 3; P,R=3,1.

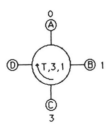

g. Upon return of frame to Station C
it's removed. Station C generates a
token at the priority just used; P,R=3,1

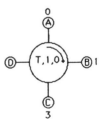

h. Station A in a priority-hold state
grabs token and changes its
priority to 1; P,R=1,0. Station A
stays in priority-hold state until
priority reduced to 0.

Legend:

Ⓐ, Ⓑ, Ⓒ, Ⓓ = stations

Numeric outside station identifier
indicates priority level.

Figure 2.6   Priority and reservation field utilization.

the prevention of a high-priority station from monopolizing the network is illustrated by station A entering a Priority-Hold state. This occurs when a station originates a token at a higher priority than the last token it generated. Once in a Priority-Hold state, the station will issue tokens that will bring the priority level eventually down to zero as a mechanism to prevent a high-priority station from monopolizing the network.

The monitor bit

The monitor bit is used to prevent a token with a priority exceeding zero or a frame from continuously circulating on the Token-Ring. This bit is transmitted as a 0 in all tokens and frames, except for a device on the network which functions as an active monitor and thus obtains the capability to inspect and modify that bit. When a token or frame is examined by the active monitor it will set the monitor bit to 1 if it was previously found to be set to 0. If a token or frame is found to have the monitor bit already set to 1 this indicates that the token or frame has already made at least one revolution around the ring and an error condition has occurred, usually caused by the failure of a station to remove its transmission from the ring or the failure of a high-priority station to seize a token. When the active monitor finds a monitor bit set to 1 it assumes an error condition has occurred. The active monitor then purges the token or frame and releases a new token onto the ring. Now that we have an understanding of the role of the monitor bit in the access control field and the operation of the active monitor on that bit, let's focus our attention upon the active monitor.

Active monitor

The active monitor is the device that has the highest address on the network. All other stations on the network are considered as standby monitors and watch the active monitor.

As previously explained, the function of the active monitor is to determine if a token or frame is continuously circulating the ring in error. To accomplish this the active monitor sets the monitor count bit as a token or frame goes by. If a destination workstation fails or has its power turned off the frame will circulate back to the active monitor, where it is then removed from the network. In the event the active monitor should fail or be turned off, the standby monitors watch the active monitor by looking for an active monitor frame. If one does not appear within seven seconds, the standby monitor that has the highest network address then takes over as the active monitor.

Frame control field

The frame control field informs a receiving device on the network of the type of frame that was transmitted and how it should be interpreted. Frames can be either logical link control (LLC) or reference physical link functions according to the IEEE 802.5 media access control (MAC) standard. A media access control frame carries network control information and responses, while a logical link control frame carries data.

The eight-bit frame control field has the format FFZZZZZZ, where FF are frame definition bits. The upper part of Table 2.3 indicates the possible settings of the frame bits and the assignment of those settings. The ZZZZZZ bits convey MAC buffering information when the FF bits are set to 00. When the FF bits are set to 01 to indicate an LLC frame, the ZZZZZZ bits are split into two fields, designated rrrYYY. Currently, the rrr bits are reserved for future use and are set to 000. The YYY bits indicate the priority of the LLC data. The lower portion of Table 2.3 indicates the value of the Z bits when used in MAC frames

Table 2.3 Frame control field subfields.

F bit settings	Assignment
00	MAC frame
01	LLC frame
10	Undefined (reserved for future use)
11	Undefined (reserved for future use)

Z bit settings	Assignment[a]
000	Normal buffering
001	Remove ring station
010	Beacon
011	Claim token
100	Ring purge
101	Active monitor present
110	Standby monitor present

[a] When F bits set to 00, Z bits are used to notify an adapter that the frame is to be expressed buffered.

to notify a Token-Ring adapter that the frame is to be expressed buffered.

Destination address field

Although the IEEE 802.5 standard is similar to Ethernet in that it supports both 16-bit and 48-bit address fields, IBM's implementation requires the use of 48-bit address fields and almost all Token-Ring networks use six-byte address fields today. The destination address field is made up of five subfields as illustrated in Figure 2.7. The first bit in the destination address identifies the destination as an individual station (bit set to 0) or as a group of one or more stations (bit set to 1). The latter provides the capability for a message to be broadcast to a group of stations.

Figure 2.7 Destination address subfields. The reserved field contains the manufacturer's identification in 22 bits represented by 6 hex digits. I/G = individual or group bit address identifier, U/L = universally or locally administered bit identifier, FAI = functional address indicator.

Universally administered address

Similar to Ethernet, the Token-Ring universally administered address is a unique address permanently encoded into an adapter's ROM. Because it is placed into ROM, it is also known as a burned-in address. The IEEE assigns blocks of addresses to each vendor manufacturing Token-Ring equipment, which insures that Token-Ring adapter cards manufactured by different vendors are uniquely defined. Some Token-Ring adapter manufacturers are assigned universal addresses that contain an organizationally unique identifier. This identifier consists of the first six hex digits of the adapter card address and is also referred to as the manufacturer identification. For example, cards manufactured by IBM will begin with the address hex 08005A or hex 10005A, whereas adapter cards manufactured by Texas Instruments will begin with the address hex 400014.

Locally administered address

A key problem with the use of universally administered addresses is the requirement to change software coding in a mainframe computer whenever a workstation connected to the mainframe via a gateway is added or removed from the network. To avoid constant software changes, locally administrated addressing can be used. This type of addressing temporarily overrides universally administrated addressing; however, the user is now responsible for insuring the uniqueness of each address.

Functional address indicator

The functional address indicator (FAI) subfield in the destination address identifies the function associated with the destination address, such as a bridge, active monitor or configuration report server.

The functional address indicator indicates a functional address when it is set to 0 and the I/G (Individual/Group) bit position is set to 1—the latter indicating a group address. This condition can only occur when the U/L (Universally/Locally administered) bit position is also set to 1 and results in the ability to generate locally administered group addresses that are called functional addresses. Table 2.4 lists the functional addresses defined by the IEEE. Currently, 14 functional addresses have been defined out of a total of 31 that are available for use, with the remaining addresses available for user definitions or reserved for future use.

Address values

The range of addresses that can be used on a Token-Ring primarily depends upon the settings of the I/G, U/L, and FAI bit positions. When the I/G and U/L bit positions are set to 00 the manufacturer's universal address is used. When the I/G and U/L bits are set to 01, individual locally administered addresses are used in the defined range listed in Table 2.4. When all three bit positions are set, this situation indicates a group address within the range contained in Table 2.5. If the I/G and U/L bits are set to 11 but the FAI bit is set to 0, this indicates that

Table 2.4 IEEE Token-Ring functional addresses.

Active Monitor	hexC000 0000 0001
Ring Parameter Server	hexC000 0000 0002
Network Server Heartbeat	hexC000 0000 0004
Ring Error Monitor	hexC000 0000 0008
Configuration Report Server	hexC000 0000 0010
Synchronous Bandwidth Manager	hexC000 0000 0020
Locate–Directory Server	hexC000 0000 0040
NETBIOS	hexC000 0000 0080
Bridge	hexC000 0000 0100
IMPL Server	hexC000 0000 0200
Ring Authorization Server	hexC000 0000 0400
LAN Gateway	hexC000 0000 0800
Ring Wiring Concentrator	hexC000 0000 1000
LAN Manager	hexC000 0000 2000
User-defined	hexC000 0000 8000 through hexC000 4000 0000

Table 2.5 Token-Ring addresses.

	Bit settings			
	I/G	U/L	FAI	Address/address range
Individual, universally administered	0	0	0/1	Manufacturer's serial no.
Individual, locally administered	0	1	0	hex4000 0000 0000 to hex4000 7FFF FFFF
Group address	1	1	1	hexC000 8000 0000 to hexC000 FFFF FFFF
Functional address	1	1	0	hexC000 0000 0001 to hexC000 0000 2000 (bit-sensitive)
All stations broadcast	1	1	1	hexFFFF FFFF FFFF
Null address	0	0	0	hex0000 0000 0000

the address is a functional address. In this situation the range of addresses is bit-sensitive, permitting only those functional addresses previously listed in Table 2.4.

In addition to the previously mentioned addresses, there are two special destination address values that are defined. An address of all 1's (hex FFFFFFFFFFFF) identifies all stations as destination stations. If a null address is used in which all bits are set to 0 (hex 000000000000), the frame is not addressed to any workstation. In this situation it can only be transmitted but not received, enabling you to test the ability of the active monitor to purge this type of frame from the network.

Source address field

The source address field always represents an individual address which specifies the adapter card responsible for the transmission. The source address field consists of three major subfields as illustrated in Figure 2.8. When locally administered addressing occurs, only 24 bits in the address field are used since the 22 manufacturer identification bit positions are not used.

Figure 2.8   Source address field. The 46 address bits consist of 22 manufacturer identification bits and 24 universally administered bits when the U/L bit is set to 0. If set to 1, a 31-bit locally administered address is used with the manufacturer's identification bits set to 0. RI = routing information bit identifier, U/L = universally or locally administered bit identifier.

The routing information (RI) bit identifier identifies the fact that routing information is contained in an optional routing information field. This bit is set when a frame will be routed across a bridge using IBM's source routing technique.

Routing information field

The routing information field (RIF) is optional and is included in a frame when the RI bit of the source address field is set. Figure 2.9 illustrates the format of the optional routing information

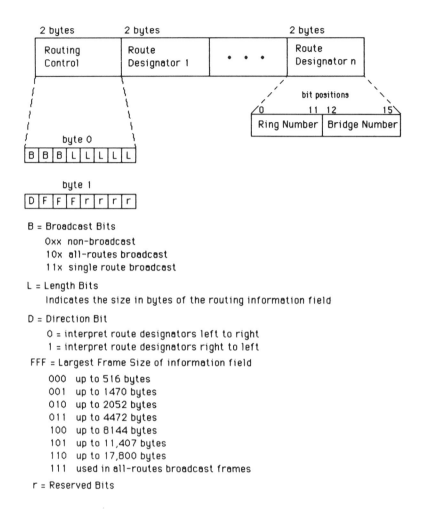

Figure 2.9 Routing information field.

field. If this field is omitted, the frame cannot leave the ring it was originated on under IBM's source routing bridging method. Under transparent bridging, the frame can be transmitted onto another ring. The routing information field is of variable length and contains a control subfield and one or more two-byte route designator fields when included in a frame, as the latter are required to control the flow of frames across one or more bridges.

The maximum length of the routing information field supported by IBM is 18 bytes. Since each routing information field must contain a two-byte routing control field, this leaves a maximum of 16 bytes available for use by up to eight route designators. As illustrated in Figure 2.9, each two-byte route designator consists of a 12-bit ring number and a four-bit bridge number. Thus, a maximum total of 16 bridges can be used to join any two rings in an Enterprise Token-Ring network.

Information field

The information field is used to contain Token-Ring commands and responses as well as carry user data. The type of data carried by the information field depends upon the F bit settings in the frame type field. If the F bits are set to 00 the information field carries media access control (MAC) commands and responses that are used for network management operations. If the F bits are set to 01 the information field carries logical link control (LLC) or user data. Such data can be in the form of portions of a file being transferred on the network or an electronic mail message being routed to another workstation on the network. The information field is of variable length and can be considered to represent the higher level protocol enveloped in a Token-Ring frame.

In the IBM implementation of the IEEE 802.5 Token-Ring standard the maximum length of the information field depends upon the Token-Ring adapter used and the operating rate of the network. Token-Ring adapters with 64 Kbytes of memory can handle up to 4.5 Kbytes on a 4 Mbps network and up to 18 Kbytes on a 16 Mbps network.

Frame check sequence field

The frame check sequence field contains four bytes which provide the mechanism for checking the accuracy of frames flowing on the network. The cyclic redundancy check data included in the frame check sequence field covers the frame control, destination address, source address, routing information and information fields. If an adapter computes a cyclic redundancy check that does not match the data contained in the frame check sequence field of a frame, the destination adapter discards the frame information and sets an error bit (E-bit) indicator. This error bit indicator, as previously discussed, actually represents a ninth bit position of the ending delimiter and serves to inform the transmitting station that the data was received in error.

Frame status field

The frame status field serves as a mechanism to indicate the results of a frame's circulation around a ring to the station that initiated the frame. Figure 2.10 indicates the format of the frame status field. The frame status field contains three subfields that are duplicated for accuracy purposes since they reside outside of CRC checking. One field (A) is used to denote if an address was recognized, while a second field (C) indicates if the frame was copied at its destination. Each of these fields is one bit in length. The third field (rr), which is two bit positions in length, is currently reserved for future use.

$$\boxed{A} \boxed{C} \boxed{r} \boxed{r} \boxed{A} \boxed{C} \boxed{r} \boxed{r}$$

A = Address-Recognized Bits
C = Frame-Copied Bits
r = Reserved Bits

Figure 2.10 Frame status field. The frame status field denotes if the destination address was recognized and if the frame was copied. Since this field is outside CRC checking its subfields are duplicated for accuracy.

Frame overhead

Unlike Ethernet which requires the use of fill characters to produce a minimum length frame of 64 bytes, there are no such restrictions on a Token-Ring frame. Although this makes the computation of the Token-Ring frame overhead more direct, this is only true when a frame does not contain a routing information field. If it does, then the length of that field, which can be up to 18 bytes, will affect the overhead of frames that traverse more than one Token-Ring network.

If we focus our attention upon frames limited to being carried on a single network, as indicated in Figure 2.3c, the overhead of a Token-Ring frame is 21 bytes. This overhead is applicable to both 4- and 16-Mbps Token-Ring networks.

Table 2.6 illustrates the overhead of Token-Ring frames as the information field varies in length from 1 to 16 384 bytes. As previously noted, the maximum information field length is 4500 bytes for a 4-Mbps Token-Ring network and 18 000 bytes for a 16-Mbps Token-Ring network.

Table 2.6 Token-Ring frame overhead.

Information field (bytes)	Frame overhead (bytes)	Percent overhead
1	21	2100.0
32	21	65.6
64	21	32.8
128	21	16.4
256	21	8.2
512	21	4.1
1 024	21	2.1
2 048	21	1.0
4 096	21	0.5
4 500	21	0.5
8 192	21	0.3
16 384	21	0.1

In examining the overhead associated with information fields whose lengths are under 512 bytes, we can express concerns with respect to network performance which are similar to those found with short Ethernet data fields. That is, if your organization is in the process of developing client–server applications, network performance can be improved by developing client–server displays and transmitting a grouping of information to the server rather than a series of short groups of data. Although there is no predefined time gap between Token-Ring frames as there is with Ethernet frames, the lower operating rate of a 4-Mbps Token-Ring frame increases the probability of poor performance with a lesser number of clients accessing a server and repeatedly transmitting short responses to server application program queries. Thus, you may be able to improve the performance of your Token-Ring network, as well as extend its ability to service additional users without degrading network performance, by designing application programs to take advantage of the structure of network frames.

3

ESTIMATING NETWORK TRAFFIC

Although there are a large number of hardware and software products that can be used to obtain network utilization information, the use of those products obviously requires an existing network. If you're planning the installation of a new network, you cannot use a performance monitor to measure network utilization until the network is established. At that time you might notice a high level of utilization, requiring the network to be subdivided through the use of a local bridge to provide a better level of performance to local area network users. Thus, it is important to understand how you can estimate network traffic and use the results of that traffic estimation process to determine whether or not you should consider the subdivision of the network via the use of a local bridge to enhance the performance level of each network segment.

In this chapter we will first focus our attention upon developing a methodology to estimate network traffic on a local area network. In doing so we will develop a traffic estimation worksheet and use that worksheet to project the average and peak traffic that could be carried on a network. Next, we will turn our attention to the typical average and peak utilization levels of Ethernet and Token-Ring networks, discussing utilization levels which, when exceeded, may indicate a decision criterion for network subdivision. This will be followed by an example which will illustrate how the use of a local bridge can make performance on each part better than if a network was not subdivided.

3.1 THE NETWORK TRAFFIC ESTIMATION PROCESS

Assuming you do not have access to monitoring equipment to analyze an existing local area network or that your network is in a planning stage, you can develop a reasonable estimate of traffic by considering the functions each network user performs. To facilitate the traffic estimation process you can group a number of network users together into a 'workstation class' category and perform your computations for a single workstation. Then, you can multiply the results of that computation by the number of workstations grouped into the specific workstation class to obtain an estimate of network traffic for a similar group of network users. You can then repeat this process for each workstation class you defined and add the traffic estimate for all workstation classes to obtain an estimate of the average traffic that will be carried on the entire network.

The traffic estimation worksheet

As mentioned at the beginning of this chapter you can expedite the traffic estimation process through the use of a worksheet. Figure 3.1 illustrates the general format of a traffic estimation worksheet you can consider to facilitate your network traffic estimation process. Prior to illustrating how you can use the worksheet, let us first review the meaning of each entry in the worksheet.

Workstation class

The workstation class identifies a specific category of local area network user. Normally you will use the occupational category of a group of persons for that entry. Typically, but not always, that entry reflects their average usage of the LAN. Examples of some common workstation classes can include secretary, engineer, accountant, payroll clerk, application programmer, and so on.

Number of stations

The number of stations entry on the worksheet permits you to indicate the number of workstations that fall into a specific workstation class. Thus, you would normally have one worksheet for each defined workstation class.

Workstation Class _____   Number of Stations _____

Activity Performed	Message Size in Bytes	Number of Frames/ Msg	Frame Size in Bytes	Frequency /Hr	Resulting Bit Rate (bps)*
				Subtotal bps =	

Total for all workstation class:

_____ = # stations _____ * subtotal bps _____ = _____

*Note:
$$\text{bit rate (bps)} = \frac{\text{frames/message * frame size * 8 bits/byte * frequency/hour}}{3600 \text{ seconds/hour}}$$

Figure 3.1 Traffic estimation worksheet.

Column entries

Turning our attention to the column entries you will note six specific column headings. The first column provides you with the ability to define the major activities performed by a workstation in the given class. Examples of major workstation activities include loading programs and data files residing on the network server, saving data files to the server, transmitting and receiving electronic mail, and directing print jobs to a network printer. Although the worksheet contains nine rows, you can add additional rows if you wish to define more than nine specific activities for a particular workstation class.

The Message Size column references the average number of bytes in a particular event performed by the defined activity. For example, suppose the transmission of electronic messages is expected to average 1800 characters. Thus, the message size in bytes would be entered as 1800.

Although several articles and technical manuals read by the author indicate the direct use of the message size, doing so results in a degree of inaccuracy. That degree of error can range in scope from a few percent for large message sizes to 30–50% or more for small size messages, due to the failure of the authors of those articles and technical manuals to consider the fact that a message must be encapsulated into one or more local area network frames and that each frame contains a number of fields that wrap around the encapsulated information. Thus, you must consider the number of frames used to carry a message as well as the frame size. Here the latter includes the overhead fields that contain the preamble (Ethernet) or starting delimiter (Token-Ring), source and destination addresses, and other frame information. As previously noted in Chapter 2, the overhead associated with Ethernet frames can vary from a low of 26 bytes when 38 or more bytes of information are carried in the data field to as many as 63 bytes when that field carries only one character of information. In comparison, a Token-Ring frame which is not routed between rings has a fixed overhead of 21 bytes.

The fifth column contained in the traffic estimation worksheet is used to place your estimate of the frequency per hour in which the row activity is performed. Even if this activity is performed only once per day, such as the remote load of a diskless workstation, you can express the frequency on an hourly basis. For example, if you expect an activity to occur once a day and project the workstation user to work an eight-hour day, then the frequency per hour becomes 1/8, or 0.125.

The last column in the traffic estimation worksheet contains the resulting bit rate computed for the specific activity entered on the row. As indicated by the footnote at the bottom of the worksheet, the bit rate in bps is determined by the following equation:

bit rate (bps) =

$$\frac{\text{frames/message} \times \text{frame size} \times 8 \times \text{frequency/hour}}{3600 \text{ seconds/hour}}$$

Once you have computed the resulting bit rate for each activity, you can sum the results of those computations to obtain the bit rate for all activities for one workstation in the class of workstations you are working with. To complete your computation for the workstation class, you would then multiply the number of workstations in the class by the summed bit rate as indicated in the lower portion of Figure 3.1. Next, you would complete the traffic estimation process by computing a total bit rate for each remaining workstation class and then sum the total for each workstation class to obtain a network traffic estimate.

Developing a network traffic estimate

Since the best way to illustrate the network traffic estimation process is by example, let's do so. Assume you want to install a Token-Ring local area network that will operate at 4 Mbps. Suppose this network is intended to support 50 design engineers; 30 technicians; 40 general support personnel in accounting, personnel, finance, sales, and marketing; 10 managers; and 10 secretaries. Thus, you would probably consider completing a series of six traffic estimation worksheets to cover each of the six general categories of users planned for the Token-Ring network.

Using the traffic estimation worksheet

Figure 3.2 illustrates the completion of a traffic estimation worksheet for the design engineer class of workstation users. In completing this worksheet it was assumed that the average design engineer will perform a core set of seven local area network functions. Those functions are listed under the Activity Performed column in Figure 3.2 and range in scope from loading a program which resides on a network server to loading and saving graphic images, sending and receiving messages, and printing both graphic images and text data on a printer to be connected to the Token-Ring network.

Required computations

To illustrate the computations used for the completion of the traffic estimation worksheet, let us consider the load program activity entry row. Here it was assumed that programs which occupy an average of 512 Kbytes of storage on the network server will be loaded five times each hour. Although this program loading frequency may appear high, many engineering programs actually consist of a series of overlays, and the loading of one program could easily result in the loading of five modules each hour as the design engineer accesses different program features in performing the design effort.

Workstation Class <u>Design Engineer</u>   Number of Stations <u>50</u>

Activity Performed	Message Size in Bytes	Number of Frames/ Msg	Frame Size in Bytes	Frequency /Hr	Resulting Bit Rate (bps)*
load program	512 K	117	4521	5	5878
load graphic image	1024 K	233	4521	3	7023
save graphic image	1024 K	233	4521	3	7023
send message	0.5 K	1	533	2	3
receive message	0.5 K	1	533	2	3
print graphic image	1024 K	233	4521	3	7023
print text data	0.5 K	1	533	4	6
				Subtotal bps =	26959

Total for all workstation class:

<u>Design Engineer</u> = # stations <u>50</u> * subtotal bps <u>26959</u> = <u>1,347,950</u>

*Note:
bit rate (bps) = <u>frames/message * frame size * 8 bits/byte * frequency/hour</u>
                                      3600 seconds/hour

Figure 3.2 Completed traffic estimation worksheet.

If the size of the program or program module loaded into the workstation is 512 Kbytes, then the actual size of the program is 512×1024 bytes per K, or 524 288 bytes.

On a 4-Mbps Token-Ring network the maximum length of the information field in a frame which contains the program data transported from the server to the workstation is 4500 bytes. Thus, 524 288 bytes in the program divided by 4500 bytes that can be carried in a frame results in 117 frames that will be required to transport the program. Although the information field is 4500 bytes, the actual frame size will be 4521 bytes since there are 21 overhead bytes in a Token-Ring frame. Based upon the preceding calculations, the resulting bit rate attributed to the load program activity becomes

bit rate (bps) =

$$\frac{117 \text{ frames} \times 4521 \text{ bytes/frame} \times 8 \text{ bits/byte} \times 5/\text{hour}}{3600 \text{ seconds/hour}} = 5878$$

In performing the previous computation, readers will note that it was not precise since the number of frames was rounded to 117 and it did not consider the fact that the last frame does not actually carry 4500 bytes. For file transfers, program loads, and print jobs, you can safely disregard the fact that the last frame used to carry an activity may have an information field whose length is less than 4500 bytes. This is because doing so results in a maximum divergence of 10 bps over an hour for the activity being computed for each occurrence of the activity. For example, 4500 bytes × 8 bits/byte results in a 4-Mbps Token-Ring information field carrying a maximum of 36 000 bits which when divided by 3600 seconds per hour is 10 bps. Thus, your activity projection would be off by a maximum of 50 bps which is less than 1%. Since you are estimating network traffic, a good rule of thumb to follow is to ignore the fact that the last frame's information field used to carry an activity may be partially filled unless the activity is performed more than 50 times per hour. The latter may represent the use of an application performed by clerical personnel entering batches of data concerning personnel file updates, corporate receipts and disbursements, and similar type work.

To further illustrate the completion of the traffic estimation worksheet illustrated in Figure 3.2, let us examine the load and save graphic image entries and the send and receive message activities. In addition, to further illustrate the computations involved in completing the worksheet, the resulting bit rate computations for each activity will also indicate the significant difference in the effect of graphic vs text information transfer on a local area network.

Graphic vs text transfer

Since the entries for loading and saving a graphic image are the same, you can compute one entry and use the resulting bit rate computation for each activity. Similarly, you can do the same for sending and receiving messages.

For each graphic image activity let us assume the image consists of a file of 1024 K bytes. Thus, the file size is 1024 × 1024 bytes per K, or 1048 576 bytes. When carried by a 4500 byte information field, this results in the use of 1048 576 bytes/4500 bytes/frame, or 233 frames, to transport the graphic image. Since there are 21 overhead bytes in each frame, the actual frame length is 4521 bytes. Based upon a frequency of three images loaded or saved per hour, each graphic image activity bit rate computation is as follows:

bit rate (bps) =

$$\frac{233 \text{ frames} \times 4521 \text{ bytes/frame } \times 8 \text{ bits/byte} \times 3/\text{hour}}{3600 \text{ seconds/hour}} = 7023$$

Now let us turn our attention to the send and receive message activities. For each activity we assumed the message size is 0.5 K, or 512 bytes. Thus, the entire message can be transported by one Token-Ring frame that has a 512-byte information field. Since there are 21 overhead bytes per Token-Ring frame, the frame size is 533 bytes. Based upon a frequency of two messages sent or received per hour, each message activity's bit rate computation becomes

bit rate (bps) =

$$\frac{1 \text{ frame} \times 533 \text{ bytes/frame} \times 8 \text{ bits/byte} \times 2/\text{hour}}{3600 \text{ seconds/hour}} = 3$$

In comparing the resulting bit rate of a graphic image activity to that of an electronic message activity, note the significant difference: here each graphic image activity has in excess of 2000 times the resulting bit rate associated with a message. Even if the message was doubled in size to 1024 bytes, the graphic image would have a bit rate 1000 times that of the message. If you consider the fact that a super-VGA monitor color graphic image can easily exceed 1 Mbytes and that most electronic mail messages are relatively short, consisting of one or two paragraphs and typically less than 100 words, this explains why electronic mail has a negligible effect upon LAN performance in comparison to the transmission of graphic images.

Returning to Figure 3.2, note that the subtotal bps of 26 959 represents the average network traffic for one workstation used by a design engineer. Since there are 50 workstations used by design engineers, the total bit rate is 26 959 × 50, or 1347 950 bps. Now that we have completed the traffic estimation worksheet for one workstation class, we would perform similar computations for each of the remaining five workstation classes. To facilitate our analysis, let us assume that the results of the computations for the six workstation classes are as summarized in Table 3.1.

Table 3.1 Projected network traffic by workstation class.

Workstation class	Bit rate (bps)
Design engineers	1 347 950
Technicians	422 500
General support personnel	238 750
Managers	83 920
Secretaries	146 750
Total estimated bit rate	2 239 870

Network utilization considerations

In examining the projected network traffic summarized in Table 3.1, note that the total bit rate of 2.23 Mbps represents a projected utilization level of 2.23/4.0, or 55%, of the available network bandwidth. Although this may not appear to be a sufficiently high level of network utilization that would result in excessive transmission delays, in actuality the transmission capability of a Token-Ring network depends upon several variables, including the number of stations on the network, the average length of frames transmitted on the network, and the total length of cable used to form the network.

Under certain variable relationships the capability of a Token-Ring network to transport data can be as low as one-half of the network's operating rate. Although Chapter 7 contains specific information concerning the development and execution of a mathematical model to determine the information-carrying capacity of a Token-Ring network, we can generalize the findings of that chapter by noting that when possible you should attempt to keep the utilization level of a Token-Ring network to a maximum of 40–50% of its operating rate. Doing so will preclude the occurrence of excessive response times. For an Ethernet local area network the utilization level should be kept to 30–40% of the network's operating rate. The rationale for an Ethernet local area network having a lower utilization level threshold than a Token-Ring network is due to the difference in the access method used by each network. Ethernet access is not predictable and can result in collisions which require a random time delay in which no station on the network can transmit data. In comparison, network access on a Token-Ring network is predictable since a station can only transmit when it is able to acquire a free token.

A second difference between the transmission capability of each network concerns the method of frame transmission used on each network. On an Ethernet network there is a minimum fixed delay period of time between frame transmissions. In comparison, transmission can occur on a Token-Ring network as soon as a station acquires a free token. Readers are referred to Chapter 6 for specific information concerning the flow of data on an Ethernet local area network.

Planning for network growth

In addition to estimating traffic that will be carried by a network, it is equally important to consider network growth. Doing so permits you to determine if a network structure will be able to accommodate a buildup in workstation usage of the network and/or an increase in network users over a period of time.

To illustrate how you can consider network growth, let us assume your organization anticipates additional hiring that will increase the design engineering staff by 5%, management personnel by 10%, and the secretarial staff by 20%. To consider the potential effect of adding workstations to the network to accommodate the additional hiring you could use a network growth worksheet similar to the one contained in Table 3.2. This worksheet was completed based upon the projected network traffic contained in Table 3.1 and the previously discussed projections for additional employees.

Table 3.2 Network growth worksheet.

Workstation class	Estimated bit rate (bps)	Projected growth rate (%)	Projected bit rate (bps)
Design engineers	1 347 950	5	1 415 348
Technicians	422 500	0	422 500
General support personnel	238 750	0	238 750
Managers	83 920	10	92 312
Secretaries	146 750	20	176 100
		Total projected bit rate	2 345 010

3.2 NETWORK MODIFICATION

Previously, it was noted that the bit rate on the Token-Ring network was projected to be approximately 55% of the available network bandwidth. Based upon the projected network growth, the bit rate is expected to increase to 2.34 Mbps, which would be 2.34/4.0, or approximately 59% of the available network bandwidth. Thus, the relatively high level of network utilization is projected to worsen over time if one network is used to provide a communications capability for both existing and anticipated employees. To alleviate potential problems associated with a high level of network utilization you should consider installing dual networks interconnected by a local bridge.

Network subdivision considerations

In examining the entries in the completed traffic estimation worksheet contained in Figure 3.2, you will note that the vast majority of network usage associated with workstations used by design engineers involves the loading of programs and graphic images as well as the saving and printing of graphic images. Thus, it appears that the requirement of design engineers to interact with other network users through the transmission and reception of electronic mail messages is relatively limited with respect to their total projected transmission on the local area network. Therefore it appears that you could safely place all design engineers on one Token-Ring network, while all other network users could be placed on a second Token-Ring network.

If the network is subdivided as previously indicated, the network supporting the design engineers would have a utilization level of 1.415/4.0, or approximately 35%, including the projected growth in the design engineering staff. The second network which would support all other network users would have a utilization level of 0.93/4.0, or approximately 23%, including projected growth in management and secretarial employees. Although this network subdivision does not provide an equal distribution of network usage, it does minimize inter-LAN communications due to the limited communications between design engineers and other organizational employees.

Figure 3.3 illustrates the resulting subdivided Token-Ring network in which it is assumed that all design engineers are placed on network A. This method of subdivision minimizes

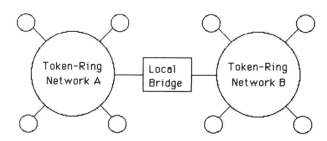

Figure 3.3 Resulting subdivided network. By placing all design engineers on Token-Ring network A, communications between network A and network B are minimized.

inter-LAN communications and reduces the forwarding rate the local bridge has to support.

As an alternative to placing all design engineers on network A, let us assume that you wish to consider network subdivision by placing half of the employees on each network. Although this would more evenly balance the utilization level of each network, what would be the effect upon inter-LAN communications? Unless you could distribute the programs and graphic images used by design engineers onto servers on each network, the design engineers on network B would require a significant amount of communications with the server located on network A. Although we did not analyze the activities of other classes of network users, we can safely assume that any subdivision in which a class of workstation users is subdivided onto two or more interconnected networks will result in a high level of inter-LAN communications unless the programs users access are located on servers on each network. Since the cost of a program license to operate on separate servers typically exceeds the cost of a program license to operate on one server, the additional cost associated with the separation or subdivision of users within a workstation class is normally not recommended. Thus, most organizations should consider the subdivision of network users based upon the class of user.

Inter- vs intra-network communications

One area which remains to be discussed concerning local area network traffic is the relationship between inter- and intra-network communications. This is especially important if your organization previously established separate local area networks and now has a requirement to interconnect those networks.

If you previously estimated traffic carried by separate networks or have access to monitoring equipment you can estimate or determine the actual data flow on separate networks. However, what can you expect to occur when you internet two or more networks together?

Unless you use a poor design philosophy and require workstations on one network to access many applications on a server on a different network, the majority of transmission will be local with respect to each LAN. In fact, the interconnection of separate networks usually results in traffic following what is commonly referred to as the 80/20 rule. That rule states that when separate networks are interconnected, intra-LAN communications will account for 80% or more of communications traffic while 20% or less of the traffic on a network will require the services of a bridge or router to flow between networks.

4

DETERMINING REMOTE BRIDGE AND ROUTER DELAYS AND BUFFER MEMORY REQUIREMENTS

One of the major problems associated with the use of remote bridges and routers is the delay those devices introduce into linked networks. This delay results from the fact that a local area network operating rate is normally an order of magnitude or higher than the wide area network operating rate used to connect LANs via the use of remote bridges or routers. A second major problem associated with the use of remote bridges and routers concerns the selection of an appropriate amount of buffer memory for installation in each device. If too little memory is installed in such devices, the probability that memory will be filled when a frame arrives for forwarding increases. This in turn results in the inability of a bridge or router to service the frame, causing the originating network station to periodically regenerate the frame or a timeout to occur which results in the termination of an existing communications session. Thus, an insufficient amount of buffer memory can result in both extended network delays as well as an increase in network traffic.

In this chapter we will first focus our attention upon the use of queuing theory to determine the delays associated with the use of remote bridges and routers. Next, we will investigate modifying the operating rate of communications circuits used to connect remote bridges and routers. Doing so will enable us to examine the effect of different communications circuit operating rates upon equipment delays, as well as to understand that beyond some operating rates further increases in the operating rate of a communications circuit have an insignificant effect upon equipment and network performance. Once we obtain an appreciation for the use of queuing theory to determine an acceptable operating rate for wide area network transmission facilities linking LANs, we will examine a related problem. That problem involves the use of queuing theory to determine whether to use single or multiple communications circuits when connecting remote LANs with respect to their ability to service frames arriving at a remote bridge or router connected to single or multiple circuits. In examining this problem we will expand our knowledge of queuing theory to cover multiple channel, single-phase queuing systems, as such systems represent the flow of data through a remote bridge or router connected to multiple communications circuits. In concluding this chapter we will turn our attention to the use of queuing theory to determine the minimum amount of buffer storage remote bridges and routers should contain to provide a predefined level of performance. In doing so we will develop a six-step approach readers can follow to select equipment with a sufficient amount of buffer storage to satisfy their specific organizational networking requirements.

4.1 WAITING LINE ANALYSIS

Queuing theory, the formal term for waiting line analysis, can be traced to the work of A. K. Erlang, a Danish mathematician. His pioneering work spanned several areas of mathematics, including the dimensioning or sizing of trunk lines to accommodate long-distance calls between telephone company exchanges. Readers are referred to the present author's book *Practical Network Design Techniques*, published by John Wiley & Sons, for specific information concerning the application of Erlang's work conducted during the 1920s to the sizing of ports on modern multiplexers and concentrators. In this chapter we will bypass Erlang's sizing work to concentrate upon the analysis of waiting lines.

Basic components

Figure 4.1 illustrates the basic components of a simple waiting line system. The input process can be considered as the arrival of people, objects, or frames of data. The service facility performs some predefined operation upon arrivals, such as collecting tolls from passengers in cars arriving at a toll booth, or converting a local area network frame into an SDLC or HDLC frame by a remote bridge or router for transmission over a wide area network transmission facility. If the arrival rate temporarily exceeds the service rate of the service facility, a waiting line known as a queue will form. If a waiting line never exists, this fact implies that the server is idle or an excessive service capacity exists.

Figure 4.1 Basic components of a simple waiting line system. When the arrival rate exceeds the service rate a waiting line or queue forms.

The waiting line system illustrated in Figure 4.1 is more formally known as a single-channel, single-phase waiting line system. The term *single channel* refers to the fact that there is one waiting line, while the term *single phase* refers to the fact that the process performed by the service facility occurs once at one location. One toll booth on a highway or a single port remote bridge connected to a local area network and a wide area network are two examples of single-channel, single-phase waiting line systems.

Figure 4.2 illustrates three additional types of waiting line systems. Here the term *multiple channel* refers to the fact that arrivals are serviced by more than one service facility and results in multiple paths or channels to those service facilities. The term *multiple phase* references the fact that arriving entities are processed by multiple service facilities.

One example of a multiple-phase service facility would be a toll road in which drivers of automobiles are serviced by several series of toll booths. Any reader who drove on the Petersburg–Richmond, VA, turnpike during the 1980s is probably well aware of the large number of 25¢ toll booths you seem to encounter every few miles. Another example of a multiple-phase

Figure 4.2 Other types of waiting line systems. In addition to single-channel, single-phase waiting line systems, other systems include multiple channel, single phase; single channel, multiple phase; and multiple channel, multiple phase.

would be the routing of data through a series of bridges and routers. Since the computations associated with multiple phase systems can become quite complex and we can analyze most networks on a point-to-point basis as a single-phase system, we will primarily restrict our examination of queuing models to single-phase systems in this chapter.

Assumptions

Queuing theory is similar to many other types of mathematical theory in that it is based upon a series of assumptions. Those assumptions are primarily focused upon the distribution of arrivals and the time required to service each arrival.

Both the distribution of arrivals and the time to service them are normally represented as random variables. The most common distribution used to represent arrivals is the Poisson distribution:

$$P(n) = \frac{\lambda^n e^{-\lambda}}{n!}$$

where:

$P(n)$ = probability of n arrivals
λ = mean arrival rate
e   = 2.718 28
$n!$ = n factorial = $n \times (n-1) \times \ldots \times 3 \times 2 \times 1$

One of the more interesting features of the Poisson process concerns the relationship between the arrival rate and the time between arrivals. If the number of arrivals per unit time is Poisson-distributed with a mean of λ, then the time between arrivals is distributed as a negative exponential probability distribution with a mean of $1/\lambda$. For example, if the mean arrival rate per 10-minute period is 3, then the mean time between arrivals is 10/3, or 3.3 minutes.

Network applications

Through the use of queuing theory or waiting time analysis, we can examine the effect of different wide area network circuit operating rates upon the ability of remote bridges and routers to transfer data between local area networks, and the effect of different levels of buffer memory on their ability to transfer data. In doing so we can obtain answers to such critical questions as 'What is the average delay associated with the use of a remote bridge or router?', 'What is the effect upon those delays by increasing the operating rate of the wide area network circuit?', 'When does an increase in the wide area network circuit's operating rate result in an insignificant improvement in bridge or router performance?', 'How much buffer memory should a remote bridge or router contain to avoid losing frames?', and similar questions. To illustrate the application and value of queuing theory to network problems, let's look at an example of its use.

Let us assume you are planning to interconnect two geographically dispersed local area networks through the use of a pair of remote bridges as illustrated in Figure 4.3. In this example a Token-Ring network at one location will be connected to an Ethernet LAN at another location. Today most remote

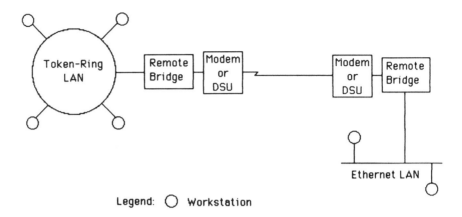

Figure 4.3 Internet consisting of two LANs connected via a pair of remote bridges. One of the most common problems facing network designers is to select an appropriate line operating rate to interconnect geographically dispersed networks.

bridges support both RS-232 and V.35 interfaces, permitting the bridge to be connected to modems or higher speed data service units (DSUs) which are used with digital transmission facilities. This opens a Pandora's box concerning the type of circuit to use to connect a pair of remote bridges, analog or digital, and the operating rate of the circuit.

Let us assume that, based upon prior knowledge obtained from monitoring the transmission between locally interconnected LANs, you determined that approximately 10 000 frames per day can be expected to flow from one network to the other network. Let us also assume that the average length of each frame was determined to be 1250 bytes.

Applying queuing theory

Based upon our assumption that 10 000 frames will flow between each LAN we must convert that frame rate into an arrival rate. In doing so let us further assume that each network is active for only eight hours per day and both networks are in the same time zone. Thus, a transaction rate of 10 000 frames per eight-hour day is equivalent to an average arrival rate of 10 000/(8×3600), or 0.347 222 frames per second. In queuing theory this average arrival rate (AR) is the average rate at which frames arrive at the service facility for forwarding across the wide area network communications circuit.

Previously we said that through monitoring it was determined that the average frame length was 1250 bytes. Since a LAN frame must be converted into a WAN frame or packet for transmission over a wide area network transmission facility, the resulting frame or packet will usually result in the addition of header and trailer information required by the protocol used to carry the LAN frame. Thus, the actual length of the wide area network frame or packet will exceed the length of the LAN frame. For our computational purposes, let us assume that 25 bytes are added to each LAN frame, resulting in the average transmission of 1275 bytes per frame.

Since the computation of an expected service time requires an operating rate, let us first assume that the wide area network communications circuit illustrated in Figure 4.3 operates at 9600 bps. Then, the time required to transmit one 1275 byte frame or packet becomes 1275 bytes/frame × 8 bits/byte÷9600 bps, or 1.0625 seconds. This time is more formally known as the expected service time and represents the time required to transmit a frame whose average length is 1250 bytes on the LAN and 1275 bytes when converted for transmission over the wide area network transmission facility. Given that the expected service time is 1.0625 seconds, we can easily compute the mean service rate (MSR). That rate is the rate at which frames entering the remote bridge destined for the other local area network are serviced and is 1/1.0625, or 0.941 1765 frames per second.

So far we have computed two key queuing theory variables, the arrival rate and the mean service rate. Note that the service rate computation was dependent upon the initial selection of a wide area network circuit operating rate which was initially selected as 9600 bps.

Figure 4.4 illustrates the results of our initial set of computations for one portion of our internet. Since we assumed that 10 000 frames per eight-hour day flow in each direction we can simply analyze one half of the internet. If our assumption was not true, you could then analyze each half and select a circuit operating rate based upon the analysis of the effect of the highest arrival rate upon LAN performance. However, if the traffic flow is not even you can simplify your computational effort by restricting your analysis to the direction of the highest frame flow. Since full duplex communications circuits operate at the same data rate in each direction, once you determine the required operating rate in one direction to support the major flow of traffic you have also determined the operating rate of the circuit.

Figure 4.4 Initial computational results. The mean service rate, MSR, or μ in queuing theory terms, depends upon the operating rate of the line.

Queuing theory designators

In examining Figure 4.4 note that queuing theory designators are indicated in parentheses. Thus, in a queuing theory book the average arrival rate of 0.347 222 transactions or frames per second would be indicated by the expression λ = 0.347 222. Similarly, the mean service rate in queuing theory books is designated by the symbol μ.

Although the mean service rate exceeds the average arrival rate, upon occasion the arrival rate will result in a burst of data which exceeds the capacity of the bridge to service frames. When this situation occurs, queues are created as the bridge accepts frames and places those frames it cannot immediately transmit into buffers or temporary storage areas. Through the use of queuing theory, we can examine the expected time for frames to flow through the bridge and adjust the circuit operating rate accordingly. In addition, we can also use queuing theory to determine the amount of buffer memory a remote bridge or router should have to minimize the potential for the loss of frames to a specific probability.

The use of remote bridges or routers can be considered to represent a single-channel, single-phase queuing model. The utilization of the service facility (p) is obtained by dividing the average arrival rate by the mean service rate. That is,

$$p = \frac{\text{AR}}{\text{MSR}} = \frac{0.347\,222}{0.941\,176\,5} = 0.3689$$

Thus, the use of a circuit operating at 9600 bps results in an average utilization level of approximately 37%. Readers should note that in queuing theory texts the preceding equation will be replaced by $p = \lambda/\mu$, where λ is the symbol used for the average arrival rate, while μ is the symbol used for the mean service rate.

Since the utilization level of the service facility (remote bridge) is AR/MSR, the probability that there are no frames in the bridge, P_0, becomes

$$P_0 = 1 - \text{AR/MSR, or} 1 - \lambda/\mu$$

For the remote bridge connected to a 9600 bps circuit we then obtain

$$P_0 = 1 - 0.37 = 0.63$$

Thus, for 63% of the time there will be no frames in the bridge's buffers awaiting transmission to the distant network.

Frame determination

For a single-channel, single-phase system the mean number of units expected to be in the system is equivalent to the average arrival rate divided by the difference between the mean service rate and the arrival rate. In queuing theory the mean or expected number of units in a system is normally designated by the letter L. Thus,

$$L = \frac{\text{AR}}{\text{MSR} - \text{AR}} = \frac{\lambda}{\mu - \lambda}$$

Returning to our networking example, we can determine the mean or expected number of frames that will be in the system, including frames residing in the bridge's buffer area or flowing down the wide area network transmission facility, as follows:

$$L = \frac{0.347}{0.941 - 0.347} = 0.585$$

Thus, on the average we can expect approximately six-tenths of a frame to reside in the bridge's buffer and on the transmission line.

If we multiply the utilization of the service facility by the expected number of units in a system we obtain the mean number of units in the queue or, in common English, the queue length. The queue length is denoted by Lq and thus becomes

$$Lq = p \times L = \frac{AR^2}{MSR(MSR - AR)} = \frac{\lambda^2}{\mu(\mu - \lambda)}$$

Again returning to our network example, we obtain

$$Lq = \frac{(0.347)^2}{0.941 \times (0.941 - 0.347)} = 0.216$$

Based upon the preceding we can expect on the average 0.216 frames to be queued in the bridge for transmission when the operating rate of the wide area network is 9600 bps and 10 000 frames per eight-hour day require remote bridging. Since we previously determined that there were 0.585 frames in the system, this means that the difference, (0.585–0.216) or 0.369 frames, is flowing on the transmission line at any particular point in time. The preceding information also provides us with data concerning the average expected utilization of the wide area network transmission facility. Since the frame length is 1275 bytes and 0.369 frames can be expected to be flowing on the circuit at any point in time, this means the line can be expected to hold 1275 bytes/frame × 0.369 frames, or 470.5 bytes. This is equivalent to 3764 bits on a line planned to operate at 9600 bps, or a circuit utilization level of approximately 39%.

Time computations

In addition to computing information concerning the expected number of frames in queues and in the system, queuing theory provides us with the tools to determine the mean time in the system and the mean waiting time. In queuing theory, the mean waiting time is designated as the variable W, while the mean waiting time in the queue is designated as the variable Wq.

The mean time in the system, W, is

$$W = \frac{1}{MSR - AR} = \frac{1}{\mu - \lambda}$$

For our bridged network example, the mean time for which a frame can be expected to reside in the system can be computed as follows:

$$W = \frac{1}{0.941 - 0.347} = 1.68 \text{ seconds}$$

By itself this tells us that we can expect an average response time of approximately 1.7 seconds for frames that must be bridged from one local area network to the other if our wide area network transmission facility operates at 9600 bps. Whether this is good or bad depends upon how you view a 1.7 second delay.

The last queuing item we will focus our attention upon is the waiting time associated with a frame being queued. That time, Wq, is equivalent to the waiting time in the system multiplied by the utilization of the service facility. That is,

$$Wq = p \times W = \frac{AR}{MSR} \times \frac{1}{(MSR - AR)} = \frac{AR}{MSR(MSR - AR)}$$

In terms of queuing theory, Wq then becomes

$$Wq = \frac{\lambda}{\mu(\mu - \lambda)}$$

One more time let us return to our bridged network example. In doing so, we obtain

$$Wq = \frac{0.347}{0.941 \times (0.941 - 0.347)} = 0.621 \text{ seconds}$$

Note that we previously determined that a frame can be expected to reside for 1.68 seconds in our bridged system, including queue waiting time and transmission time. Since we computed queue waiting time to be 0.621 seconds, the difference between the two, 1.68–0.621, or approximately 1.06 seconds, is the time required to transmit a frame over the 9600 bps wide area network transmission facility.

4.2 DETERMINING AN OPTIMUM LINE OPERATING RATE

Although we could recompute each of the previously computed variables based upon different line operating rates, we can just as easily write a program to perform such tedious operations.

Program QUEUE.BAS

Figure 4.5 lists the statements of a BASIC language program appropriately named QUEUE.BAS. The execution of this program is shown in Figure 4.6 which displays the values for eight queuing theory parameters based upon line speeds ranging from 4800 bps to 1.536 Mbps. The latter line speed represents the effective operating rate of a T1 circuit, since 8000 bps of the 1.544 Mbps operating rate of that circuit is used for framing and is not available for the actual transmission of data.

```
REM PROGRAM QUEUE.BAS
CLS
REM AR=arrival rate
REM MSR=mean service rate
REM L=mean (expected) number of frames in system
REM Lq=mean number of frames in queue
REM W=mean time (s) in system
REM Wq=mean waiting time (s)
REM EST= expected service time
transactions = 10000          'transactions per day
avgframe = 1275               'average frame size
hrsperday = 8
AR = transactions / (8 * 60 * 60)
DATA 4800,9600,19200,56000,64000,128000,256000,384000,768000,1536000
FOR i = 1 TO 10
READ linespeed(i)
est(i) = avgframe * 8 / linespeed(i)
msr(i) = 1 / est(i)
utilization(i) = AR / msr(i)
prob0(i) = 1 - (AR / msr(i))
L(i) = AR / (msr(i) - AR)
Lq(i) = AR ^ 2 / (msr(i) * (msr(i) - AR))
W(i) = 1 / (msr(i) - AR)
Wq(i) = AR / (msr(i) * (msr(i) - AR))
NEXT i
PRINT "Line Speed  EST    MSR      Po        p        L        Lq        W        Wq"
FOR i = 1 TO 10
PRINT USING " #######  #.#### ###.## "; linespeed(i); est(i); msr(i);
PRINT USING " #.#####    .#####"; prob0(i); utilization(i);
PRINT USING "  #.#####  #.#####  #.#####   #.#####"; L(i); Lq(i); W(i); Wq(i)
NEXT i
PRINT
PRINT "where:"
PRINT
PRINT " EST= expected service time  MSR = mean service rate"
PRINT " Po=probability of zero frames in the system  p = utilization"
PRINT " L= mean number of frames in system Lq = mean number in queue"
PRINT " W= mean waiting time in system  Wq = mean waiting time in queue"
```

Figure 4.5 Program listing of QUEUE.BAS.

```
Line Speed  EST    MSR     Po        p       L        Lq        W        Wq
     4800  2.1250   0.47  0.26215  .73785  2.81457  2.07672  8.10596  5.98096
     9600  1.0625   0.94  0.63108  .36892  0.58459  0.21567  1.68363  0.62113
    19200  0.5313   1.88  0.81554  .18446  0.22618  0.04172  0.65141  0.12016
    56000  0.1821   5.49  0.93676  .06324  0.06751  0.00427  0.19444  0.01230
    64000  0.1594   6.27  0.94466  .05534  0.05858  0.00324  0.16871  0.00934
   128000  0.0797  12.55  0.97233  .02767  0.02846  0.00079  0.08196  0.00227
   256000  0.0398  25.10  0.98617  .01383  0.01403  0.00019  0.04040  0.00056
   384000  0.0266  37.65  0.99078  .00922  0.00931  0.00009  0.02681  0.00025
   768000  0.0133  75.29  0.99539  .00461  0.00463  0.00002  0.01334  0.00006
  1536000  0.0066 150.59  0.99769  .00231  0.00231  0.00001  0.00666  0.00002
```

where:

```
EST= expected service time  MSR = mean service rate
Po=probability of zero frames in the system  p = utilization
L= mean number of frames in system Lq = mean number in queue
W= mean waiting time in system  Wq = mean waiting time in queue
```

Figure 4.6 Execution results of program QUEUE.BAS.

Utilization level vs line speed

In examining the values of the queuing parameters listed in Figure 4.6, let us focus our attention upon the utilization level, P, and the mean waiting time in the queue, Wq. At 4800 bps note that the utilization level is approximately 74%, while the waiting time in the queue is almost six seconds! Clearly, linking the two local area networks via remote bridges operating at 4800 bps provides an unacceptable waiting time due to the high utilization level of the remote bridge.

As the line speed connecting the remote bridges is increased, each bridge is able to service frames at a higher processing rate. Since the average arrival rate is fixed, increasing the line operating rate should lower the utilization level of the bridge as well as the time for which a frame resides in the queue. Our expectation is verified by the results of the execution of QUEUE.BAS shown in Figure 4.6. Note that, as expected, both the utilization level and mean waiting time in the queue decrease as the line speed increases.

Selecting an operating rate

At the beginning of this chapter it was mentioned that queuing theory could be used to determine the operating rate of transmission lines for linking remote bridges and routers. In actuality, such usage will not produce a 'magic number'. Instead, the use of queuing theory can provide you with a range of values from which you can make a logical decision. For example, returning to Figure 4.6, a line operating rate of 4800 bps is clearly unacceptable. However, what can we say concerning an operating rate of 9600 bps, 19 200 bps, 56 000 bps, and so on?

To provide some 'food for thought', Figure 4.7 graphs the probability of a bridge containing zero frames (e.g., having empty buffers) and the utilization level of the bridge based upon the 10 line operating rates that were considered. Note that at a line operating rate above the 56–64 Kbps range, further reductions in the utilization level of the bridge and an increase in the probability of zero frames in the system is essentially insignificant. Thus, you would more than likely restrict your line operating rate to a maximum of 56–64 Kbps in this example. From Figure 4.6, note that doing so only marginally decreases the waiting time in the queue from 0.12 seconds at 19 200 bps to 0.012 seconds at 56 Kbps. Thus, if you were fairly certain that your application would not grow, you would probably install an analog leased line operating at 19 200 bps as the cost of that line is normally less than the cost of a digital line operating at 56 or 64 Kbps. If you expect further growth in the use of remote bridges, you would probably install a more expensive 56 or 64 Kbps digital line.

Summary

To correctly apply queuing theory to interconnecting local area networks you must first obtain knowledge about the number of transactions and the average frame size of each transaction that will flow to the other network. Once this is accomplished you must estimate the growth in the average frame size to reflect the addition of header and trailer information required by the wide area protocol to carry your LAN frame. This then provides you with the ability to compute the average arrival rate of frames as well as the mean service rate of a remote bridge or router. Then, you can easily compute the additional queuing parameters previously discussed in this section and recalculate those parameters for different transmission line operating rates whose examination will enable you to select an appropriate operating rate to interconnect your LANs.

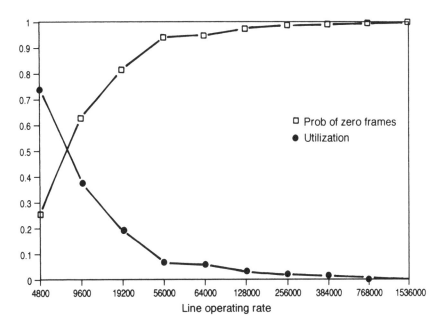

Figure 4.7 Probability of zero frames vs utilization.

4.3 EXAMINING SINGLE AND MULTIPLE COMMUNICATIONS CIRCUITS

One of the more common decisions facing a network designer is whether to use single or multiple communications circuits when connecting remote local area networks via the use of bridges or routers. Obviously, from a reliability point of view multiple circuits are preferable to the use of a single circuit. However, from a performance point of view, are two circuits, each with one-half the transmission capacity of a single circuit, better than the use of a single transmission path? This is the question that will be examined in this section, while leaving an investigation of the gain in availability and reliability of multiple circuits over single circuits for Chapter 5.

Comparing the use of single and dual port equipment

Figure 4.8 illustrates the use of single and dual port remote bridges to connect an Ethernet local area network to a distant Token-Ring local area network. Suppose the single port remote bridges are connected to data service units (DSUs) that operate at 19 200 bps, while the multiport remote bridges are connected to two DSUs, each operating at 9600 bps. Although each pair

a. Using single port remote bridges

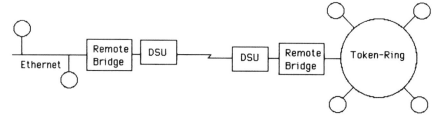

b. Using multiport remote bridges

Legend:
DSU = data service unit
○ = network stations

Figure 4.8 Comparing the use of a: single- and b: dual-port (or multiport) remote bridges. If the single communications circuit in a operates at twice the data rate of each of the multiple circuits shown in b, does each network configuration provide an equal level of service?

of bridges has access to an aggregate transmission capacity of 19 200 bps, does the use of single and dual transmission paths in which the single path operates at twice the rate of each dual transmission path provide an equivalent level of service? To answer this question let us return to the use of queuing theory. In doing so, let us assume that the number of transactions estimated to flow between local area networks is 21 600 per eight-hour day. Let us also assume that the average frame size, including communications framing for transmission, is 1200 bytes.

Single circuit

The single circuit communications link illustrated in Figure 4.8a more formally represents what is known as an M/M/1 queuing system.

Notation

The notation M/M/1 is actually a shorthand abbreviation of the form A/B/C which is used by queuing theorists to describe queuing problems. The letter used in the A position represents the statistical characteristics of the arrival rate of items to be serviced, such as customers approaching a teller or frames flowing to a bridge. A probability density function (pdf), such as the Poisson pdf, is typically used to describe a customer arrival rate. One of the most commonly used pdf's is the exponential pdf, which is denoted as M in queuing theory shorthand notation. The exponential pdf is defined as

$$p(t) = \lambda e^{-\lambda t}$$

This pdf is equivalent to saying that arriving customers behave as if they were not aware of each other's existence, i.e., occur randomly. Thus, the arrival process is a process without memory and the shorthand abbreviation M used to denote an exponential arrival rate actually references the fact that the arrivals are 'memoryless'.

Readers should note that systems with an exponential interarrival distribution result in a Poisson arrival rate distribution. In fact, the probability that exactly n customers will arrive in a period of time t is given by the equation

$$P(n,t) = \frac{\lambda t^n e^{-\lambda t}}{n!}$$

The above equation is the Poisson probability function. Thus, an exponential interarrival time distribution which is memoryless and denoted in queuing shorthand notation by M is generated by a Poisson process in which the arrival of any customer is independent of the arrival of previous customers.

Returning to the A/B/C notation format used to describe a queuing problem, B represents the statistical characteristics of the server. A server which operates without regard to the length of a queue, e.g., does not get tired, has its behavior described by an exponential service time distribution. Thus, such servers are also 'memoryless' and the letter M is used in position B to describe the characteristics of our server. Finally, the letter C in the queuing problem shorthand description format represents the number of servers. Thus, the numeric 1 was used in our shorthand queuing abbreviation for position C to complete our description of the queuing model in Figure 4.8a.

Computations

Based upon 21 600 transactions occurring in an eight-hour day, the arrival rate becomes

$$\lambda = \frac{21\,600}{8 \times 3600} = 0.75 \text{ per second}$$

Since it was assumed that the average frame size is 1200 bytes, the expected service time when the line operates at 19 200 bps becomes $1200 \times 8/19\,200$, or 0.5 seconds. Thus, the service rate becomes

$$\mu = \frac{1}{\text{expected service time}} = \frac{1}{0.5} = 2 \text{ per second}$$

The utilization of the server (p) is the arrival rate divided by the service rate. Thus,

$$p = \frac{\lambda}{\mu} = \frac{0.75}{2} = 0.375$$

The probability that there are no frames in the system (P_0) is one minus the utilization. Thus,

$$P_0 = 1 - \frac{\lambda}{\mu} = 1 - 0.375 = 0.625$$

Let us continue and compute the mean number of frames expected in the system (L) and the mean length of the queue (Lq). Doing so, we obtain

$$L = \frac{\lambda}{\mu - \lambda} = \frac{0.75}{2 - 0.75} = 0.6$$

$$Lq = \frac{\lambda^2}{\mu(\mu - \lambda)} = \frac{p^2}{1 - p} = \frac{(0.375)^2}{1 - 0.375} = 0.225$$

Thus, we can expect 0.6 frames to be in the system, while 0.225 frames on the average will be in the queue. Now let us focus our attention upon waiting times, the mean time waiting (Wq) and the mean time waiting in the system (W). Those two parameters are computed as follows:

$$Wq = \frac{\lambda}{\mu(\mu - \lambda)} = \frac{0.75}{2(2 - 0.75)} = 0.3 \text{ seconds}$$

$$W = \frac{1}{\mu - \lambda} = \frac{1}{2 - 0.75} = 0.8 \text{ seconds}$$

Note that the difference between the average waiting time in the system of 0.8 seconds and the average waiting time in the queue of 0.3 seconds is 0.5 seconds. That time is exactly the expected service time for a 1200-byte frame to be carried on a 19 200-bps transmission circuit. Now that the basic queuing-related performance elements for the single path circuit have been computed, let's focus our attention upon the use of dual transmission circuits.

Dual circuits

The dual transmission path illustrated in Figure 4.8 represents an M/M/2 queuing system in which the numeric indicates there are two servers or, in our example, two channels or circuits.

Although you will normally think of a server as a device with memory which enables queues to form, you can also treat each circuit as a server. In doing so, each remote bridge then provides the buffer memory for the formation of queues for service or placement onto each communications circuit. Here the use of two channels or communications circuits can be considered to represent a queuing system which is more formally referred to as a multiple channel, single phase queuing system.

Computations

In computing the queuing parameters note that the arrival rate of 0.75 frames per second remains the same. However, since each circuit now operates at 9600 bps the expected service time is 1200 bytes × 8 bits/byte÷9600 bytes, or 1 second. Thus, the service rate, μ, is 1/1, or 1 frame per second per transmission line.

For a multiple-channel, single-phase system, utilization is computed as follows, where s is the number of servers

$$p = \frac{\lambda}{s\mu} = \frac{0.75}{2 \times 1} = 0.375$$

So far everything appears to be equivalent between a single transmission line and two lines in which each of the latter operate at one-half the rate of the former.

In a multiple-channel, single-phase queuing system, the probability that there are no frames in the system (P_0) is determined using the following formula:

$$P_0 = \frac{1}{\sum\limits_{n=0}^{s-1} \left[\frac{(\lambda/\mu)^n}{n!} \right] + \frac{(\lambda/\mu)^s}{s!(1-\lambda/s\mu)}}$$

where s represents the number of servers and $n!$ and $s!$ represent n and s factorial. The results of the computations for our two-server model to obtain the probability that there are no frames in the system are as follows:

$$P_0 = \frac{1}{1 + 0.75 + \frac{(0.75)^2}{2(1 - 0.75/2)}}$$

$$= \frac{1}{1 + 0.75 + 0.45} = \frac{1}{2.2} = 0.45$$

This means that there is a 45% probability that both servers do not contain any frames at any point in time.

Now that P_0 has been computed, we can use our prior computations in equations developed for multiple-channel, single-phase systems for other queuing parameters of interest. Those four parameters, Lq, L, W, and Wq, are computed as follows:

$$Lq = \frac{P_0(\lambda/\mu)^2 p}{S!(1 - p)^2} = \frac{0.45(0.75)^2 \times 0.365}{2(1 - 0.375)^2} = 0.1215$$

$$L = Lq + \frac{\lambda}{\mu} = 0.1215 + \frac{0.75}{1} = 0.8715$$

$$Wq = \frac{Lq}{\lambda} = \frac{0.1215}{0.75} = 0.162$$

$$W = Wq + \frac{1}{\lambda} = 0.162 + 1 = 1.162$$

General observations

So far we have made a number of computations. Now let's compare our previous computations and use the comparison between single and dual server models to make some general observations. Table 4.1 compares the queuing computations for the single and dual communications paths illustrated in Figure 4.8.

Table 4.1 Comparing single and dual path queuing values.

Parameter	Single path	Dual path
Arrival rate (λ)	0.75	0.75
Service rate (μ)	2	1
Utilization (p)	0.375	0.375
Probability no frame in system (P_0)	0.625	0.45
Mean number of frames in system (L)	0.6	0.87
Mean length of queue (Lq)	0.225	0.12
Mean time in system (W)	0.3	1.162
Mean waiting time (Wq)	0.8	0.162

In comparing the entries in Table 4.1 between the single and dual path scenarios, let's first focus our attention upon P_0, the probability that there is no frame in the system. Note that the single path has a higher probability that there is no frame in the system than the dual path. The reason for this can be explained by examining Figure 4.9 which indicates how transmission gaps can occur on two paths each operating at a fraction of a single path.

Suppose a 2400-byte frame arrives at a server connected to a single 19 200-bps data circuit. As indicated in the upper portion of Figure 4.9, one 19 200-bps circuit could transmit the first 2400-byte frame in precisely one second. If a second frame shows up precisely one second later, the first frame would have been transmitted and the transmission of the second frame can then commence. If a second frame shows up just a fraction of a second after the first frame, the second frame will be queued for transmission. Then, once the first frame is transmitted the second frame will immediately follow the first frame. In fact, the second frame can arrive at any time up to one second after the first frame without a transmission gap occurring. Now consider

Legend:
xxxxx   transmission time for first 2400-byte frame
=====   transmission time for second 2400-byte frame

Figure 4.9 Transmission gaps commonly occur on multiple circuits. The use of multiple circuits operating at a fraction of the operating rate of a single circuit can be expected to result in more transmission gaps for the same frame arrival rate to a service facility.

a similar situation in which two 2400-byte frames arrive one second apart at a bridge connected to two communications circuits. The first frame requires two seconds for transmission, while the second 9600-bps circuit is unoccupied for one second until the second frame arrives and is then transmitted on the second circuit since the first circuit is occupied. Since there is no way to split a frame between circuits, there is no way to fill the gap that occurred. The one-second gap illustrated in the lower portion of Figure 4.9 represents half the longest duration gap based upon the previous assumptions. If a second frame arrived two seconds after the first, a two-second period of time would occur in which one circuit was not occupied. Similarly, if the second frame followed the first by 0.5 seconds, the gap would be reduced to a 0.5 second duration. As illustrated from this example, the use of two queuing systems each with half the capacity of a single system will almost always have a lower level of performance due to the higher probability of occurrence of transmission gaps.

By comparing the single and dual path queuing values listed in Table 4.1, readers will note that there are other significant differences between a single circuit operating at X bps and two circuits each operating at $X/2$ bps. For example, the mean number of frames in the system less the mean length of the queue tells us the mean number of frames on the circuit or circuits. Here the use of a single path would result in 0.6 − 0.225, or 0.375 frames, while the dual path would have 0.87 − 0.12, or 0.75 frames. This means that the mean number of frames in a two-circuit system is twice the number of frames found in a single circuit system—a situation we would intuitively expect.

Another area of difference between the single and dual circuit configurations concerns waiting times. Although the mean waiting time in the queue is less for a two-circuit configuration as it provides two paths for transmitting frames, its mean system time considerably exceeds that of a single path system. What this tells us is that the use of multiple circuits provides a larger 'moving storage' facility for frames than a single circuit system; however, the end result is that although queuing time (Wq) is reduced, the total time in the system (W) is increased. Thus, discounting availability considerations, a choice between a single circuit operating at X bps and two circuits each operating at $X/2$ bps should be made in favor of the single circuit.

Program QUEUE2.BAS

To facilitate computations associated with two-channel, single-phase queuing systems, the program QUEUE.BAS was modified. The results of that modification provide queuing statistics for a two-channel, single phase queuing system for line rates ranging from 4800 bps to 1.536 Mbps. This program modification was renamed QUEUE2.BAS and its statements are listed in Figure 4.10. In addition to revising the program to compute two-channel, single-phase queuing system statistics, the program was also modified to accept daily transactions, operational hours per day, and an average frame size as user input.

Figure 4.11 illustrates an example of the results of executing QUEUE2.BAS. In this example the program was executed using 21 600 transactions per eight-hour day with an average frame size of 1200 bytes.

```
REM PROGRAM QUEUE2.BAS
CLS
PRINT "PROGRAM QUEUE2.BAS - STATISTICS FOR TWO CHANNEL SINGLE PHASE QUEUE"
PRINT
REM AR=arrival rate
REM MSR=mean service rate
REM L=mean (expected) number of frames in system
REM Lq=mean number of frames in queue
REM W=mean time (s) in system
REM Wq=mean waiting time (s)
REM EST= expected service time
INPUT "Enter transactions per day      : "; transactions
INPUT "Enter operational hours per day : "; hrs
INPUT "Enter average frame size        : "; frame
AR = transactions / (hrs * 60 * 60)
DATA 4800,9600,19200,56000,64000,128000,256000,384000,768000,1536000
FOR I = 1 TO 10
READ linespeed(I)
est(I) = frame * 8 / linespeed(I)
MSR(I) = 1 / est(I)
UTILIZATION(I) = AR / (2 * MSR(I))
PROBO(I) = 1 / (1 + (AR / MSR(I)) + (AR / MSR(I)) ^ 2 / (2 * (1 - (AR / (2 * MSR(I))))))
Lq(I) = PROBO(I) * (AR / MSR(I)) ^ 2 * UTILIZATION(I)
Lq(I) = Lq(I) / (2 * (1 - UTILIZATION(I)) ^ 2)
L(I) = Lq(I) + AR / MSR(I)
Wq(I) = Lq(I) / AR
W(I) = Wq(I) + 1 / MSR(I)
NEXT I
PRINT "Line Speed  EST    MSR    Po       p       L       Lq      W       Wq"
FOR I = 1 TO 10
PRINT USING " #######  #.#### ###.## "; linespeed(I); est(I); MSR(I);
PRINT USING " #.##### #.#####"; PROBO(I); UTILIZATION(I);
PRINT USING "  #.##### #.##### #.#####   #.#####"; L(I); Lq(I); W(I); Wq(I)
NEXT I
PRINT
PRINT "where:"
PRINT
PRINT " EST= expected service time  MSR = mean service rate"
PRINT " Po=probability of zero frames in the system  p = utilization"
PRINT " L= mean number of frames in system Lq = mean number in queue"
PRINT " W= mean waiting time in system  Wq = mean waiting time in queue"
```

Figure 4.10 Program listing QUEUE2.BAS.

```
PROGRAM QUEUE2.BAS - STATISTICS FOR TWO CHANNEL SINGLE PHASE QUEUE

Enter transactions per day      : ? 21600
Enter operational hours per day : ? 8
Enter average frame size        : ? 1200
Line Speed  EST     MSR     Po       p        L        Lq       W        Wq
      4800  2.0000   0.50   0.14286  0.75000  3.42857  1.92857  4.57143  2.57143
      9600  1.0000   1.00   0.45455  0.37500  0.87273  0.12273  1.16364  0.16364
     19200  0.5000   2.00   0.68421  0.18750  0.38866  0.01366  0.51822  0.01822
     56000  0.1714   5.83   0.87919  0.06429  0.12910  0.00053  0.17214  0.00071
     64000  0.1500   6.67   0.89349  0.05625  0.11286  0.00036  0.15048  0.00048
    128000  0.0750  13.33   0.94529  0.02813  0.05629  0.00004  0.07506  0.00006
    256000  0.0375  26.67   0.97227  0.01406  0.02813  0.00001  0.03751  0.00001
    384000  0.0250  40.00   0.98142  0.00938  0.01875  0.00000  0.02500  0.00000
    768000  0.0125  80.00   0.99067  0.00469  0.00938  0.00000  0.01250  0.00000
   1536000  0.0063 160.00   0.99532  0.00234  0.00469  0.00000  0.00625  0.00000

where:

EST= expected service time  MSR = mean service rate
Po=probability of zero frames in the system  p = utilization
L= mean number of frames in system Lq = mean number in queue
W= mean waiting time in system  Wq = mean waiting time in queue

Press any key to continue
```

Figure 4.11   Execution results of program `QUEUE2.BAS`.

4.4 BUFFER MEMORY CONSIDERATIONS

Most bridges and routers are modular devices whose feature selection list may contain more entries than a restaurant menu. Among the features from which you can normally select is a series of different memory modules which govern the buffer area in which frames can be queued when the frame arrival rate temporarily exceeds the service rate of the bridge or router.

Although the cost of memory has significantly declined over the past few years, a wild guess can still be costly from an operational perspective. Thus, we will conclude this chapter by examining how you can use queuing theory to make an educated estimate of the amount of buffer memory that should be installed in remote bridges and routers.

Average memory

Previously, we determined the mean length of the queue, denoted as Lq. By multiplying the value of Lq by the average frame size you can determine the average amount of buffer memory that will be occupied. Unfortunately, this results in the average amount of buffer memory required and means that half the time more memory will be required. Thus, to obtain a more meaningful mechanism to estimate buffer memory requirements you must consider another method to determine the use of buffer memory. That method is obtained by computing the probability of different numbers of frames in a queuing system.

Using probability

The probability of n units (P_n) in a single-channel, single-server system is obtained from the following formula:

$$P_n = \left(\frac{\lambda}{\mu}\right)^n \left(1 - \frac{\lambda}{\mu}\right) = p^n(1 - p)$$

The probability of k or more units ($P_{n>k}$) in a single-channel, single-server system is given by the formula

$$P_{n>k} = \left(\frac{\lambda}{\mu}\right)^k = p^k$$

To illustrate the use of the preceding formulas, let us return to our prior computations in which the utilization level was determined to be 0.375. Figure 4.12 lists the statements of a BASIC program labeled UNITS.BAS which you will use to compute the value of $P(N)$ and $P(N>K)$ as N and K vary from 0 to 20 for a single-channel, single-server system. This program was written to accept any server utilization level, which provides you with the ability to use it to satisfy the computational requirements associated with a specific situation.

Figure 4.13 illustrates the results obtained from the execution of the program UNITS.BAS with a server utilization level of 0.375, which is equivalent to 37.5%. In examining the data listed in Figure 4.13, note the relationship between $P(N)$ and $P(N>K)$. That is, $P(N)$ provides the probability for a specific number of units or (for our example) frames in a system, while $P(N>K)$ provides the probability that there are K or more units in the system. Thus, there is a 62.5% probability that there are no frames in the system ($P(N=0)$), while as expected there is a probability of unity that there are zero or more frames in the system. Although you could use either column of probabilities

```
REM PROGRAM UNITS.BAS TO COMPUTE PROBABILITY OF N UNITS IN SYSTEM
REM AND PROBABILITY OF K OR MORE UNITS IN SYSTEM
CLS
PRINT "PROGRAM TO COMPUTE PROBABILITY OF N UNITS AND K OR MORE UNITS IN SYSTEM"
DIM P(20), K(20)
INPUT "Enter utilization level of server"; P
PRINT "PROBABILITY OF N UNITS    PROBABILITY K OR MORE UNITS"
PRINT "  N      P(N)              K        P(N>K)"
FOR N = 0 TO 20
P(N) = P ^ N * (1 - P)
K(N) = P ^ N
PRINT USING "### #.########            ###   #.########"; N; P(N); N; K(N)
NEXT N
END
```

Figure 4.12   Program listing of UNITS.BAS.

```
PROGRAM TO COMPUTE PROBABILITY OF N UNITS AND K OR MORE UNITS IN SYSTEM
Enter utilization level of server? .375
PROBABILITY OF N UNITS    PROBABILITY K OR MORE UNITS
  N      P(N)              K        P(N>K)
  0 0.62500000            0    1.00000000
  1 0.23437500            1    0.37500000
  2 0.08789063            2    0.14062500
  3 0.03295898            3    0.05273438
  4 0.01235962            4    0.01977539
  5 0.00463486            5    0.00741577
  6 0.00173807            6    0.00278091
  7 0.00065178            7    0.00104284
  8 0.00024442            8    0.00039107
  9 0.00009166            9    0.00014665
 10 0.00003437           10    0.00005499
 11 0.00001289           11    0.00002062
 12 0.00000483           12    0.00000773
 13 0.00000181           13    0.00000290
 14 0.00000068           14    0.00000109
 15 0.00000025           15    0.00000041
 16 0.00000010           16    0.00000015
 17 0.00000004           17    0.00000006
 18 0.00000001           18    0.00000002
 19 0.00000001           19    0.00000001
 20 0.00000000           20    0.00000000
```

Figure 4.13   Execution results of program UNITS.BAS with a server utilization
level of 0.375.

as a decision criterion for determining the amount of buffer space you need in your bridge or router, you will shortly note that the second column provides a more direct value.

In attempting to determine the size of the buffer space you require, the question you must answer is 'How big should the buffer be to satisfy a predefined probability level of X%?'. Then, once you define the probability level you can answer the question. For example, assume you want a buffer size big enough to store 99.9% of the occurrences when the arrival rate exceeds the service rate. To accomplish this you can directly use the right-hand columns listed in Figure 4.13 in which the probability of K or more units is tabulated for K varying from 0 to 20. To obtain a level of 99.9% of the occurrences is equivalent to not being able to handle 0.1% of the occurrences, which would be displayed as 0.001 in the second P column of Figure 4.13. Note that when K is 7, $P(N>K)$ is 0.001 0428 4, or slightly more than 0.1%. Thus, you must select K equal to 8 to satisfy your requirement for handling 99.9% of the occurrences in which the frame arrival rate exceeds the service rate of the bridge or router. Thus, through the use of Figure 4.13 you would want the bridge or router to be capable of storing or queuing up to eight frames. Since the frame length was defined as 1200 bytes, your memory storage requirement becomes 1200 bytes/frame $\times$ 8 frames, or 9600 bytes for this particular situation.

Six-step approach

The steps required to determine queuing storage requirements can be summarized as follows:

(1) Determine the average frame arrival and average server service rates.
(2) Determine the utilization level of the server.
(3) Determine the level of service you want the server to provide with respect to storing or queuing frames for transmission when the frame arrival rate exceeds the server's service rate.
(4) Determine the probability of K or more units in the system for a range of values.
(5) Determine the probability that $N>K$, where K represents the level of service you want the server to provide, and locate that value in the computed range of probabilities.

Then, extract the value of *K* which represents the number of frames that must be queued.

(6) Multiply the average or maximum frame length by the number of frames that must be queued. Note that multiplying by the average frame length results in obtaining the average buffer storage required for a given level of probability, while multiplying by the maximum frame length supported by your LAN results in obtaining a buffer storage value which will satisfy all situations for the predefined probability level.

Considering the maximum frame size

Although the first five steps are relatively self-explanatory, the sixth step may be confusing to some readers. Thus, let's take a moment prior to proceeding and focus our attention upon the last step.

Previously you determined that your bridge or router should have 9600 bytes of buffer storage to queue 99.9% of the occurrences in which the frame arrival rate exceeds the server's service rate. In actuality, the prior computation was based upon an average frame length of 1200 bytes. Thus, the amount of buffer storage you computed satisfies an average of 99.9% of the occurrences in which the frame arrival rate exceeds the server's service rate. If you wish to obtain a buffer storage value which fully satisfies your probability requirement, you must then use the maximum frame size supported by the local area network you are using or anticipate installing. For example, if you are using an Ethernet or IEEE 802.3 LAN, its maximum frame size is 1500 bytes (excluding overhead preamble and addressing and CRC bytes), while the use of a 4-Mbps or 16-Mbps Token-Ring LAN would result in a maximum frame size of 4500 or 18 000 bytes, respectively.

Program QVU.BAS

To facilitate performing another set of calculations, the program QVU.BAS was developed. Figure 4.14 lists the statements contained in this program which computes the buffer requirements for Ethernet and 4- and 16-Mbps Token-Ring networks based upon different server utilization levels ranging up to 99.0%. Readers can easily modify this program to

```
REM PROGRAM QVU.BAS TO COMPARE QUEUE LENGTH VERSUS SERVER UTILIZATION LEVEL
CLS
FRAME = 1500
LPRINT "ANALYSIS OF BUFFER STORAGE REQUIREMENTS"
LPRINT "MAXIMUM ETHERNET FRAME SIZE = 1500 BYTES"
LPRINT "MAXIMUM 4MBPS TOKEN-RING FRAME SIZE  = 4500 BYTES"
LPRINT "MAXIMUM 16MBPS TOKEN-RING FRAME SIZE =18000 BYTES"
LPRINT
LPRINT "UTILIZATION   LENGTH OF QUEUE     BUFFER REQUIREMENTS IN BYTES"
LPRINT " PERCENT         IN FRAMES         ETHERNET    4MBPS T-R   16MBPS T-R"
FOR P = 0! TO .9 STEP .1
LQ = P ^ 2 / (1 - P)
B = INT(LQ * FRAME + .99)
T4 = INT(LQ * 4500 + .99)
T16 = INT(LQ * 18000 + .99)
LPRINT USING "###.##          ####.###         ########"; P * 100; LQ; B;
LPRINT USING "  ######## ########"; T4; T16
NEXT P
FOR P = .91 TO .99 STEP .01
LQ = P ^ 2 / (1 - P)
B = INT(LQ * FRAME + .99)
T4 = INT(LQ * 4500 + .99)
T16 = INT(LQ * 18000 + .99)
LPRINT USING "###.##          ####.###         ########"; P * 100; LQ; B;
LPRINT USING "  ######## ########"; T4; T16
NEXT P
END
```

Figure 4.14 Program listing of QVU.BAS.

obtain buffer requirements for other server utilization levels or to slightly expand frame sizes to better reflect the overhead associated with transmitting a frame using a specific wide area network protocol.

Figure 4.15 illustrates the results obtained from the execution of QVU.BAS. In examining the data in Figure 4.15 note that the length of the queue in terms of frames is relatively small until the server's utilization level exceeds 70%. Thereafter, it rapidly increases and will approach infinity as the utilization level approaches 100%. Thus, you can use the data in Figure 4.15 to determine if you really need to continue further and compute $P(N>K)$ or if you can simply estimate that at the level of server utilization the buffer requirements are so small that just about every bridge and router should have a sufficient amount of buffer memory. For example, suppose your server's utilization level was 50% and your organization operates a 4-Mbps Token-Ring LAN. Figure 4.15 indicates an average buffer storage requirement of 2250 bytes, infinitesimally small in comparison to the 32 or 64 Kbytes of buffer storage included in most remote

```
ANALYSIS OF BUFFER STORAGE REQUIREMENTS
MAXIMUM ETHERNET FRAME SIZE = 1500 BYTES
MAXIMUM 4MBPS TOKEN-RING FRAME SIZE  = 4500 BYTES
MAXIMUM 16MBPS TOKEN-RING FRAME SIZE =18000 BYTES
```

UTILIZATION	LENGTH OF QUEUE	BUFFER REQUIREMENTS IN BYTES		
PERCENT	IN FRAMES	ETHERNET	4MBPS T-R	16MBPS T-R
0.00	0.000	0	0	0
10.00	0.011	17	50	200
20.00	0.050	75	225	900
30.00	0.129	193	579	2315
40.00	0.267	400	1200	4800
50.00	0.500	750	2250	9000
60.00	0.900	1350	4050	16200
70.00	1.633	2450	7350	29400
80.00	3.200	4800	14400	57601
91.00	9.201	13802	41406	165621
92.00	10.580	15870	47611	190441
93.00	12.356	18534	55601	222403
94.00	14.727	22090	66270	265080
95.00	18.050	27075	81225	324900
96.00	23.040	34560	103680	414720
97.00	31.363	47045	141135	564540
98.00	48.020	72030	216090	864359
99.00	98.009	147015	441043	1764171

Figure 4.15 Execution results of program QVU.BAS.

bridges and routers. Thus, without further analysis to compute $P(N>K)$ you could safely conclude that a 32 Kbyte buffer area should be sufficient for $P(N>99.9)$. However, since many readers will probably feel more comfortable by selecting a probability level and performing the six-step sequence previously listed, Appendix A summarizes values of $P(N)$ and $P(N>K)$ for different server utilization levels ranging from $P=10\%$ to $P=95\%$ in increments of 5%.

Summary

Although a variety of queuing concepts were examined in this chapter, it is most important to remember several concepts which govern the application of queuing theory to networking. One concept is that as the level of utilization of a server increases, its queue length increases. A second concept worth remembering is the fact that as the level of utilization for a single server system exceeds 50% queues become more observable to whatever process you are performing. A third concept worth noting is the fact that as the level of utilization of a server approaches 100%, the length of a queue increases dramatically and will eventually approach infinity.

Table 4.2 gives the queue length for different utilization levels of a single-phase, single-channel system. Note that at a 50% utilization level, the mean queue length is 0.5; however, at a 70% level of utilization, the queue length is more than three times the 50% figure. Also note that an increase in utilization from 70 to 80% results in a doubling of the mean queue length, while an increase in utilization from 80 to 91% results in the length of the queue nearly tripling. Figure 4.16 graphically illustrates the same data. In examining Figure 4.16, it is important to remember that the mean queue length is directly related to the mean waiting time and explains why most network managers, analysts, and designers should consider modifying a network facility when its utilization level exceeds 50%.

Table 4.2 Queue length vs server utilization.

Utilization (%)	Length of queue
0	0.000
10	0.011
20	0.050
30	0.129
40	0.267
50	0.500
60	0.900
70	1.633
80	3.200
91	9.201
92	10.580
93	12.356
94	14.727
95	18.050
96	23.040
97	31.363
98	48.020
99	98.009

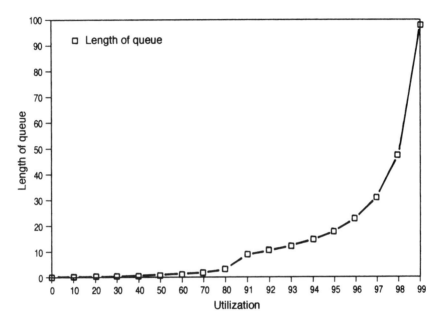

Figure 4.16 Queue length vs server utilization for a single-channel, single-phase system.

DETERMINING THE AVAILABILITY LEVEL OF SINGLE AND MULTIPLE PORT DEVICES

In Chapter 4 the application of queuing theory to determining transmission delays through remote bridges and routers was examined. As noted in that chapter, you can use queuing theory to compare the use of single versus multiple circuits used to connect remote bridges and routers. In doing so, the use of single and multiple circuits were examined from a performance perspective, leaving until this chapter a discussion of availability issues.

One of the more important decisions network managers face is determining whether to install single or multiple port devices such as remote bridges and routers. By understanding how availability is computed one can obtain the knowledge necessary to determine whether or not the cost of additional bridge ports, communications equipment, and transmission facilities is worthwhile with respect to the additional level of network availability obtained through the use of different communications configurations.

5.1 AVAILABILITY

In the same way that 'one person's passion is another person's poison', there are different ways in which you can look at and define availability. Thus, to alleviate any possibility of confusion, let us first define the term as it relates to both components and systems. Once this is accomplished, we can examine its applicability to different local area network communications configurations.

Component availability

The availability of an individual component can be expressed in two ways which are directly related to one another. First, as a percentage, availability can be defined as the operational time of a device divided by the total time, with the result multiplied by 100. This is indicated by the following equation:

$$A\% = \frac{\text{operational time}}{\text{total time}} \times 100$$

where $A\%$ is availability expressed as a percentage.

For example, consider a leased line modem which normally operates continuously 24 hours per day. Over a one-year period of time let us assume the modem failed once and required eight hours to repair. During the year the modem was available for use for 365 days $\times$ 24 hours/day less 8 hours, or 8752 hours. Thus, the modem was operational for 8752 hours during a period of 8760 hours. Using our availability formula we obtain

$$A\% = \frac{8752}{8760} \times 100 = 99.91\%$$

MTBF and MTTR

Now let's define two commonly used terms and discuss their relationship to operational time and total time. The first term, Mean Time Before Failure (MTBF), is the average operational time of a device prior to its failure. Thus, MTBF is equivalent to the operational time of a device.

Once a device fails, you must initiate actions to effect its repair. The interval from the time the device fails until the time the device is repaired is known as the time to repair, and the average of each repair time is known as the Mean Time To Repair (MTTR). Since the total time is MTBF + MTTR, we can rewrite our availability formula as follows:

$$A\% = \frac{\text{MTBF}}{\text{MTBF} + \text{MTTR}} \times 100$$

It is important to remember the M in MTBF and MTTR as you must use the average or mean time before failure and average or mean time to repair. Otherwise, your calculations are subject to error. For example, if your modem failure occurred halfway through the year, you might be tempted to assign 4380 hours to the MTBF. Then, you would compute availability as

$$A\% = \frac{4380}{4380 + 8} \times 100 = 99.91\%$$

The problem with the above computation is the fact that only one failure occurred, which results in the MTBF not actually representing a mean. Although the computed MTBF is correct for one particular modem, as sure as the sun rises in the East, the MTBF would be different for a second modem, different again for a third modem, and so on. Thus, if you are attempting to obtain an availability level for a number of devices installed or to be installed you, in effect, will compute an average level of availability through the use of an average MTBF. Thus, the next logical question is how to obtain average MTBF information for a communications device. Fortunately, many vendors provide MTBF information for the products they manufacture that you can use instead of waiting for a significant period of time to obtain appropriate information. Concerning the MTTR, this interval is also provided by the manufacturer but normally requires a degree of modification to be realistic.

Most manufacturers quote a MTTR figure based upon the time required to repair a device once a repair person is on site. Thus, you must consider the location where your equipment is to be installed and travel time from a vendor's location to your location. If your organization has a maintenance contract which guarantees a service call within a predefined period after notification of an equipment failure, you can use that time period and add it to the MTTR. For example, assume the specification sheet for a vendor's modem listed a MTBF of 16 500 hours and a MTTR of two hours. If you anticipate installing the modem in Macon, Georgia, and the nearest vendor service office is located in the northern suburbs of Atlanta, you would probably add four to six hours to the MTTR time. This addition would reflect the time required for a repair person in Atlanta to receive notification that he or she should service a failed device in Macon, complete his or her work in Atlanta, and travel to the site in Macon. While this may not be significant when a MTBF exceeds one year, suppose your equipment location was Boise, Idaho, and the modem vendor used next-day delivery to ship a replacement modem, in effect, repairing by replacement. In this situation you may have to add 24 hours or more to the time required to swap modems to obtain a more realistic MTTR value.

System availability

In communications a system is considered to represent a collection of devices connected through the use of one or more transmission facilities which form a given topology. Thus, to determine the availability of a system you must consider the availability of each device and transmission facility as well as the overall topology of the system. Concerning the latter, the structure of the system in which components are connected in serial or in parallel will affect the overall availability of a system. To illustrate the effect of topology upon system availability, several basic local area network structures in which devices are connected in series and in parallel will be examined.

Devices connected in series

The top portion of Figure 5.1 illustrates the connection of n components in series. In this and subsequent illustrations a component will be considered to represent either a physical network device or a transmission facility connecting two devices. Thus, the boxes labeled A_1, A_2, and A_3 could represent the availability of a modem (A_1), the availability of a leased line (A_2), and the availability of a second modem (A_3).

The availability of n components connected in series is computed by multiplying together the availabilities of each of the n individual components. Mathematically, this is expressed as follows for n components:

$$A = \prod_{i=1}^{n} A_i$$

To illustrate the computation of a system in which components are arranged in series, consider the Token-Ring network

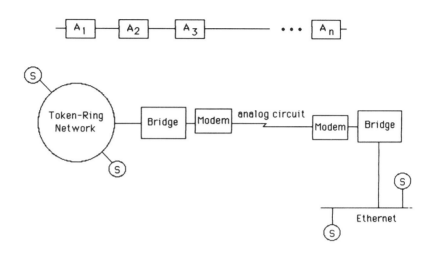

Figure 5.1 Network components in series. The availability of a system in which components are connected in series is obtained by multiplying together the availabilities of each of the individual components.

connected to an Ethernet LAN via the use of two remote bridges and a pair of analog modems. This networking system is illustrated in the lower portion of Figure 5.1.

Let us assume that each remote bridge has a MTBF of one year, or 8760 hours, and any failure would be corrected by the manufacturer shipping a replacement unit to each location where a bridge is installed. Thus, we might assume a worst-case MTTR of 48 hours to allow for the time between reporting a failure and the arrival and installation of a replacement unit. Similarly, let us assume a MTBF of 8760 hours and a MTTR of 48 hours for each modem. For the transmission line most communications carriers specify a 99.5% level of availability for digital circuits, so using a slightly lower level of 99.4% for an analog circuit would appear to be reasonable. Based upon the preceding formula, the availability of the communications system, A_S, which enables a user on a Token-Ring network to access the Ethernet network and vice versa via a pair of single port bridges, then becomes

$$A_S\% = \left[(\text{Bridge}_A)^2 \times (\text{Modem}_A)^2 \times \text{Line}_A \right] \times 100$$

where:

  Bridge_A is the availability level of each bridge
  Modem_A is the availability level of each modem

$Line_A$ is the availability level of the analog circuit connecting the two locations

Since the availability of each component equals the MTBF divided by the sum of the MTBF and the MTTR, we obtain

$$A_S\% = \left[\left(\frac{8760}{8808}\right)^2 \times \left(\frac{8760}{8808}\right)^2 \times 0.994\right] \times 100 = 97.25\%$$

This means that for approximately 2.75% of the time (100 − 97.25) in which an attempt is made to use the communications system the failure of one or more components will render the system inoperative.

Devices connected in parallel

Figure 5.2a illustrates n devices connected in parallel. If only one device out of n is required to provide communications at any point in time, then the availability of the system as a percentage becomes

$$A_S\% = \left(1 - \prod_{i=1}^{n}(1 - A_i)\right) \times 100$$

For example, assume two devices each having an availability level of 99% are operated in parallel. Then, the availability level of the resulting parallel system becomes

$$A_S\% = \left(1 - \prod_{i=1}^{2}(1 - A_i)\right) \times 100$$

Substituting, we obtain

$$A_S\% = \left[1 - (1 - 0.99) \times (1 - 0.99)\right] \times 100 = 99.99\%$$

Since communications within and between networks normally traverse multiple components, the use of parallel transmission paths normally involves multiple components on each path. Figures 5.2b and 5.2c illustrate two methods by which alternative paths could be provided to connect the Token-Ring and Ethernet networks together.

a. n components connected in parallel

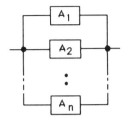

b. Using dual single port bridges

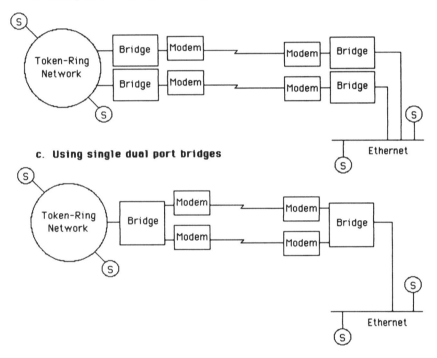

c. Using single dual port bridges

Figure 5.2   Connecting devices in parallel.

Readers should note that transparent bridging supported by Ethernet networks precludes the use of closed loops which physically occur through the use of dual bridges or multiport bridges illustrated in Figures 5.2b and 5.2c. However, if we assume that only one path operates at a single point in time, the use of two paths in which one only becomes active if the other becomes inactive is supported by transparent bridging.

In the topology illustrated in Figure 5.2b duplicate remote bridges, modems, and transmission paths were assumed to be installed. In Figure 5.2c it was assumed that your organization could obtain a very reliable remote bridge and preferred to expend funds on parallel communications circuits and modems, since the failure rate of long-distance communications facilities normally exceeds the failure rate of equipment.

For simplicity, let's assume that the availability level of each component illustrated in Figure 5.2b is 0.9. For each parallel path you can consider the traversal of the path to encounter five components: two bridges, two modems, and the communications line. Thus, the upper path containing five devices in series would have an availability level of $0.9 \times 0.9 \times 0.9 \times 0.9 \times 0.9$, or $0.590\,49$. Similarly, the lower path would have a level of availability of $0.590\,49$. Thus, you have now reduced the network structure to two parallel paths, each having an availability level of $0.590\,49$. If A_1 is the availability level of path 1 and A_2 is the availability level of the second path, the system availability, A_S becomes

$$A_S\% = \left(1 - \prod_{i=1}^{2} (1 - A_i)\right) \times 100$$

Thus:

$$A_S\% = [1 - (1 - A_1)(1 - A_2)] \times 100$$

Simplifying the above equation by multiplying the terms and substituting $0.590\,49$ for A_1 and A_2, you obtain

$$A_S\% = [A_1 + A_2 - (A_1 \times A_2)] \times 100 = 83.23\%$$

Mixed topologies

Now let's focus our attention upon the network configuration illustrated in Figure 5.2c in which a common bridge at each LAN location provides access to duplicate transmission facilities. To compute the availability of this communications system, you can treat each bridge as a serial element, while the two modems and the communications line between each modem represent parallel routes of three serial devices.

Figure 5.3 illustrates how you can consider the communications system previously illustrated in Figure 5.2c as a sequence of serial and parallel elements. By combining groups of serial and parallel elements you can easily compute the overall level of availability for the communications system as indicated in the four parts of Figure 5.3. In Figure 5.3a the three

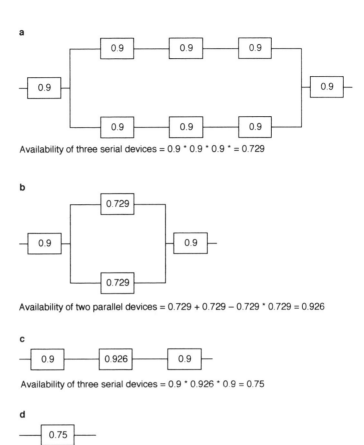

Figure 5.3 Computing the availability of a mixed serial and parallel transmission system.

serial elements of each parallel circuit are combined, including the two modems and communications line, to obtain a serial availability level of $0.9 \times 0.9 \times 0.9$, or 0.729. Next, in Figure 5.3b the two parallel paths are combined to obtain a joint availability of $0.729 + 0.729 - (0.729 \times 0.729)$, or 0.926. Finally, in Figure 5.3c the joint availability of the parallel transmission paths is treated as a serial element with the two bridges, obtaining a system availability of 0.75 (Figure 5.3d). Note that at a uniform 90% level of availability for each device the use of single bridges in place of dual bridges lowers the system availability by approximately 8%. That is, the system availability obtained through the use of dual single-port bridges illustrated in Figure 5.2b was computed to be 83.23%; in comparison, the system availability obtained from the use of single dual-port bridges illustrated in Figure 5.2c was determined to be 75%.

Dual hardware vs dual transmission facilities

In the above calculations, assuming a uniform component availability of 0.9 (90%), the system availability of the dual network illustrated in Figure 5.2b was computed to be 83.23%, while the availability of the network illustrated in Figure 5.2c was computed to be 75%. Although the difference in availability of over 8% could probably justify the extra cost associated with dual bridges for organizations with critical applications, what happens to the difference in the availability of each network as the availability level of each component increases?

Table 5.1 compares the system availability for the use of single multiport and parallel single port bridge networks as component availability increases from 0.9 to 0.999. In examining the entries in Table 5.1 you will note that the difference between the availability level of each network decreases as component availability increases. In fact, the 8% difference at a component availability level of 0.9 decreases to under 4% at a component availability level of 0.98 and to under 2% at a component availability level of 0.99. Since most modern communications devices have a component availability level close to 0.999, which, by the way, usually exceeds the availability level of a transmission facility by 0.005, the use of dual bridges instead of multiport bridges may be limited to increasing network availability by 0.1%. Thus, you must balance the gain in availability against the cost of redundant bridges.

Table 5.1 System availability comparison.

	System availability	
Component availability	Single multiport bridge	Parallel single-port bridges
0.90	0.7505	0.8323
0.91	0.7778	0.8586
0.92	0.8049	0.8838
0.93	0.8318	0.9073
0.94	0.8582	0.9292
0.95	0.8841	0.9488
0.96	0.9094	0.9659
0.97	0.9337	0.9800
0.98	0.9571	0.9908
0.99	0.9792	0.9976
0.999	0.9980	0.9999

Concerning cost, although bridges vary considerably with respect to features and price, at the middle of 1993 their average price was approximately $4000. In comparison, the incremental cost of a dual port bridge over that of a single port bridge was typically less than $500. Since you require two bridges to link geographically separated networks, the cost difference between the use of dual single-port bridges and single dual-port bridges is approximately (4000 − 500) × 2, or $7000. Thus, in this example you would have to decide if an increase in network availability by approximately 0.1% is worth $7000.

If your organization operates a reservation system in which a minute of downtime could result in the loss of thousands of dollars of revenue, the additional cost would probably be most acceptable. If your organization uses your network for interoffice electronic mail transmission, you might prefer to save the $7000 and use single dual-port bridges instead of dual single-port bridges. This is because a gain of 0.1% of availability based upon an eight-hour workday with 22 workdays per month would only provide 2.1 additional hours of availability per year. At a cost of approximately $3500 per hour for the additional availability, it might be more economical to simply delay non-urgent mail and use the telephone for urgent communications.

5.2 AUTOMATING AVAILABILITY COMPUTATIONS

As we noted in the first section of this chapter, the computation of system availability can be reduced to a series of computations for devices in series and in parallel. To facilitate the computations involved in determining serial and parallel component availability, the program AVAIL.BAS was developed. Figure 5.4 lists the statements in that BASIC language program.

Program AVAIL.BAS

The program AVAIL.BAS can be used to compute the availability levels for components connected in series or in parallel. In fact, by selecting the program's BOTH option, the program will first compute the availability level of components connected in series and then compute the availability level of components connected in parallel.

To facilitate data entry the program permits you to enter data in either of two ways. You can enter data concerning the availability level of individual components as a percentage value or you can enter MTBF and MTTR values. For either data entry method the program accepts a maximum of 10 component availability level values which should be more than sufficient for essentially all network configurations. In the event you require the computation of more than 10 component availability level values, you can easily modify AVAIL.BAS. To do so you would simply add a DIM statement at the beginning of the program which would contain a value for each array used in the program that reflects the highest number of components you intend to analyze. Since BASIC automatically dimensions all arrays to 10 elements, no DIM statement was required in AVAIL.BAS.

Program execution

Since the best way to illustrate the use of a computer program is to execute the program, let's do so. In doing so, let's assume our network configuration consists of two sets of five components connected in series, with each set routed parallel to the other set of components. Let us also assume that we have component availability expressed as a percentage for one set of components and as MTBF and MTTR data for the second set of components.

Figure 5.5 illustrates the execution of AVAIL.BAS to compute the availability of five serially connected components when the availability for each component is specified as a percentage. In this example, it was assumed that four components each had an availability level of 99.9%, while one component had an availability level of 99.85%. As noted at the bottom of Figure 5.5, the availability level of the five devices in series was computed to be 99.45%.

Figure 5.6 illustrates the execution of the program AVAIL.BAS to compute the availability of five serially connected components when you wish to use and have available MTBF and MTTR data. In this example it was assumed that four network components each had an MTBF of 8000 hours and an MTTR of 24 hours. Concerning the latter, it was assumed that repair is accomplished by replacement and that your organization uses Express Mail, Federal Express, or a similar overnight service to deliver a new device which will be used to replace a failed device. Since your presumed experience is that the average

Figure 5.4 Program listing of AVAIL.BAS.

```
REM PROGRAM AVAIL.BAS
CLS
PRINT "PROGRAM AVAIL.BAS TO COMPUTE AVAILABILITY LEVELS"
PRINT
PRINT "INDICATE COMPUTATIONS DESIRED "
PRINT "      S)ERIAL"
PRINT "      P)ARALLEL"
PRINT "      B)OTH SERIAL AND PARALLEL"
AGN:    INPUT "ENTER THE TYPE OF COMPUTATIONS DESIRED          : ", COMP$
IF COMP$ <> "S" AND COMP$ <> "P" AND COMP$ <> "B" THEN GOTO AGN:
IF COMP$ = "B" THEN TRY$ = "A"
IF COMP$ = "B" THEN COMP$ = "S"
GOSUB DENTER
IF COMP$ = "S" THEN GOSUB SCOMPUTE
IF COMP$ = "P" THEN GOSUB PCOMPUTE
IF TRY$ = "A" THEN COMP$ = "P"
IF TRY$ = "A" THEN GOSUB DENTER
IF TRY$ = "A" THEN GOSUB PCOMPUTE
STOP
DENTER:
        IF COMP$ = "P" THEN GOTO PAR
        INPUT "ENTER NUMBER OF COMPONENTS IN SERIAL -MAX 10    : ", C
        IF COMP$ = "S" THEN GOTO SER
PAR:    INPUT "ENTER NUMBER OF COMPONENTS IN PARALLEL - MAX 10 : ", C
SER:    PRINT
        PRINT "HOW DO YOU WANT TO ENTER DATA ?"
        PRINT "AS  P)ERCENT E.G. 12.5"
        PRINT "AS  M)TBF AND MTTR"
        INPUT "ENTER DATA ENTRY METHOD -P OR M                 : ", D$
        IF D$ <> "P" AND D$ <> "M" THEN GOTO DENTER
        IF D$ = "M" GOTO MENTRY
        FOR I = 1 TO C
        PRINT "FOR COMPONENT"; I;
        INPUT "ENTER PERCENT AVAILABILITY        : ", A(I)
        A(I) = A(I) / 100
        NEXT I
        RETURN
MENTRY:
        FOR I = 1 TO C
        PRINT "FOR COMPONENT"; I;
        INPUT "ENTER MTBF AND MTTR VALUES        : ", MTBF(I), MTTR(I)
        A(I) = MTBF(I) / (MTBF(I) + MTTR(I))
        NEXT I
        RETURN
SCOMPUTE:
        IF COMP$ = "P" GOTO PCOMPUTE
        PROD = 1
        FOR I = 1 TO C
        PROD = PROD * A(I)
        NEXT I
        PRINT USING "AVAILABILITY OF ## "; C;
        PRINT USING " DEVICES IN SERIES = ##.#####"; PROD * 100
        RETURN
PCOMPUTE:
        PROD = 1
        FOR I = 1 TO C
        PROD(I) = (1 - A(I))
        PROD = PROD * PROD(I)
        NEXT I
        AVAIL = 1 - PROD
        PRINT USING "AVAILABILITY OF ##"; C;
        PRINT USING " DEVICES IN PARALLEL = ##.#####"; AVAIL * 100
        RETURN
END
```

```
PROGRAM AVAIL.BAS TO COMPUTE AVAILABILITY LEVELS

INDICATE COMPUTATIONS DESIRED
        S)ERIAL
        P)ARALLEL
        B)OTH SERIAL AND PARALLEL
ENTER THE TYPE OF COMPUTATIONS DESIRED          : S
ENTER NUMBER OF COMPONENTS IN SERIAL -MAX 10    : 5

HOW DO YOU WANT TO ENTER DATA ?
AS   P)ERCENT E.G. 12.5
AS   M)TBF AND MTTR
ENTER DATA ENTRY METHOD -P OR M                 : P
FOR COMPONENT 1 ENTER PERCENT AVAILABILITY      : 99.9
FOR COMPONENT 2 ENTER PERCENT AVAILABILITY      : 99.9
FOR COMPONENT 3 ENTER PERCENT AVAILABILITY      : 99.85
FOR COMPONENT 4 ENTER PERCENT AVAILABILITY      : 99.9
FOR COMPONENT 5 ENTER PERCENT AVAILABILITY      : 99.9
AVAILABILITY OF  5   DEVICES IN SERIES = 99.45120
```

Figure 5.5 Execution of program AVAIL.BAS to compute availability of serially connected devices using the percent availability method of data entry.

time from failure notification to the replacement of the failed device is 24 hours, you used 24 for each of four MTTR values. For one component you used an MTBF of 720 hours and an MTBR of two hours. This availability setting is representative of

```
PROGRAM AVAIL.BAS TO COMPUTE AVAILABILITY LEVELS

INDICATE COMPUTATIONS DESIRED
        S)ERIAL
        P)ARALLEL
        B)OTH SERIAL AND PARALLEL
ENTER THE TYPE OF COMPUTATIONS DESIRED          : S
ENTER NUMBER OF COMPONENTS IN SERIAL -MAX 10    : 5

HOW DO YOU WANT TO ENTER DATA ?
AS   P)ERCENT E.G. 12.5
AS   M)TBF AND MTTR
ENTER DATA ENTRY METHOD -P OR M                 : M
FOR COMPONENT 1 ENTER MTBF AND MTTR VALUES      : 8000,24
FOR COMPONENT 2 ENTER MTBF AND MTTR VALUES      : 8000,24
FOR COMPONENT 3 ENTER MTBF AND MTTR VALUES      : 720,2
FOR COMPONENT 4 ENTER MTBF AND MTTR VALUES      : 8000,48
FOR COMPONENT 5 ENTER MTBF AND MTTR VALUES      : 8000,48
AVAILABILITY OF  5   DEVICES IN SERIES = 97.94843
```

Figure 5.6 Execution of program AVAIL.BAS to compute availability of serially connected devices using the MTBF and MTTR method of data entry.

many digital transmission lines, since there are 24×30, or 720 hours in a 'typical' month, and one two-hour failure provides an approximate 99.7% level of line availability. As indicated at the bottom of Figure 5.6, the availability level of this second set of five devices connected in series was computed to be 97.95%.

Now that you have determined the availability level of each set of serially connected devices you can compute system availability by treating each resulting computed value as two devices in parallel. Thus, you can use AVAIL.BAS one more time to compute the system availability level of your two sets of five serially connected devices. To do so you will execute AVAIL.BAS and select the parallel computation option.

Figure 5.7 illustrates the execution of AVAIL.BAS in which the parallel option was selected. Since your previous executions of AVAIL.BAS resulted in two availability levels expressed as a percentage, you will now select the percent data entry method for the parallel component computations. As indicated in Figure 5.7, entering the results of the previous serial availability levels results in an availability level of 99.988 74%. This represents the system availability level of the two sets of five serially connected components whose individual availability levels were previously specified. As indicated by this short example, you can use the program AVAIL.BAS to simplify the computations associated with different network structures, since those structures can be considered to represent a mixture of devices connected in series or in parallel.

```
PROGRAM AVAIL.BAS TO COMPUTE AVAILABILITY LEVELS

INDICATE COMPUTATIONS DESIRED
     S)ERIAL
     P)ARALLEL
     B)OTH SERIAL AND PARALLEL
ENTER THE TYPE OF COMPUTATIONS DESIRED          : P
ENTER NUMBER OF COMPONENTS IN PARALLEL - MAX 10 : 2

HOW DO YOU WANT TO ENTER DATA ?
AS  P)ERCENT E.G. 12.5
AS  M)TBF AND MTTR
ENTER DATA ENTRY METHOD -P OR M                 : P
FOR COMPONENT 1 ENTER PERCENT AVAILABILITY      : 99.4512
FOR COMPONENT 2 ENTER PERCENT AVAILABILITY      : 97.94843
AVAILABILITY OF  2 DEVICES IN PARALLEL = 99.98874
```

Figure 5.7 Execution of program AVAIL.BAS to compute availability of parallel connected devices.

6

ESTIMATING ETHERNET NETWORK PERFORMANCE

In Chapters 4 and 5 several models were developed and exercised to compute transmission delays, buffer memory requirements, and availability levels associated with the use of remote bridges and routers. In Chapter 4 you did not have to consider the types of local area networks to be connected other than noting that transmission delays and buffer memory requirement computations were based upon several average frame sizes assumed to be flowing on a network. This enabled us to develop general models that can be tailored to a specific network environment by exercising a model with the appropriate frame size monitored or estimated to be carried by a network. In Chapter 5, it was noted that the availability levels of different network configurations are independent of the types of local area networks to be connected. In this chapter we will begin to focus our attention upon the performance requirements of specific types of local area networks by examining the CSMA/CD access protocol. This will enable us to construct a model which reflects the transfer of frames on an Ethernet network at different levels of network utilization. This in turn will provide us with a foundation for computing the maximum frame forwarding rate required to be supported by a bridge or router connected to an Ethernet network to ensure the device is fully capable of supporting the maximum level of Ethernet transmission. As in preceding chapters, a BASIC language program will be developed and executed to facilitate exercising the mathematical models developed in this chapter.

6.1 CSMA/CD NETWORK PERFORMANCE

Ethernet is a carrier sense multiple access with collision detection (CSMA/CD) network. Each station on the network listens for a carrier and attempts to transmit data when it senses the absence of that signal. Unfortunately, two stations may attempt to transmit data simultaneously, resulting in the occurrence of a collision. Even when one station thinks there is no carrier, it is quite possible that a carrier signal is propagating down the transmission path. Thus, a station transmitting data when its sampling of the line indicates the absence of a carrier may also result in a collision.

Because of the random nature of collisions, Ethernet bus performance is not deterministic and performance characteristics and message transmission delays are not predictable. However, over a period of time you can determine average and peak utilization, data elements which you may use to split one Ethernet LAN into two or more LANs via the use of bridges to increase individual network performance.

Determining the network frame rate

The top portion of Figure 6.1 illustrates the IEEE 802.3 (Ethernet) frame format. In this illustration the seven-byte preamble field and the one-byte start of frame delimiter field are combined into a common eight-byte preamble field for simplicity. In actuality, the preamble field used by Ethernet is an eight-byte sequence of alternating 1's and 0's, while the IEEE 802.3 frame format uses a seven-byte preamble field of alternating 1's and 0's. The one-byte start of frame delimiter field used in IEEE 802.3 frames follows a seven-byte preamble field and the sequence of alternating 1's and 0's but ends with two set bits instead of the 1 and 0 used in the Ethernet preamble field. Since computations required to estimate Ethernet network and bridge and router performance are based upon frame length and not frame composition, the use of a common eight-byte preamble field, while not technically correct from a frame composition basis, does not affect our computations. As indicated by the tabulation of frame field lengths in the lower portion of Figure 6.1, the frame size can vary from a minimum of 72 to a maximum of 1526 bytes.

Under Ethernet and 802.3 standards there is a dead time of 9.6 μs between frames. Using the frame size and dead time

Preamble	Destination Address	Source Address	Length or Type	Data	Frame Check Sequence
8	6	6	2	$46 \leq n \leq 1500$	4

Frame Size (bytes)

Field	Minimum Size Frame	Maximum Size Frame
Preamble	8	8
Destination Address	6	6
Source Address	6	6
Length or Type	2	2
Data	46	1500
Frame Check Sequence	4	4
Total Size	72	1526

Figure 6.1 IEEE 802.3 (Ethernet) frame format.

between frames you can compute the maximum number of frames per second that can flow on an Ethernet network. For our example, let us assume we have a 10 Mbps LAN, such as a 10BASE-2, 10BASE-5, or 10BASE-T network. Here the bit time then becomes $1/10^7$ seconds or 100 ns.

Now let us assume all frames are at the maximum length of 1526 bytes. Then, the time per frame becomes

$$9.6 \ \mu s + 1526 \ \text{bytes} \times \frac{8 \ \text{bits}}{\text{byte}} \times \frac{100 \text{ns}}{\text{bit}} = 1.23 \ \text{ms}$$

Since one 1526-byte frame requires 1.23 ms, then in one second there can be 1/1.23 ms or approximately 812 maximum-sized frames. Thus, the maximum transmission rate on an Ethernet network is 812 frames per second when information is transferred in 1500-byte units within a sequence of frames. One example of a situation in which data would be transferred in 1500-byte units is when a workstation downloads a file from a server or transfers a file to another workstation or to a server. When this type of data transfer occurs, the data fields of a large number of sequential frames would be filled to their maximum size of 1500 bytes. If the last portion of the file being transferred is less than 1500 bytes, then the data field of the last frame used to transport the file would be less than 1500 bytes in length.

Now that the maximum number of frames that can traverse an Ethernet network when the data field is at its maximum size has been determined, let's compute the frame rate when the data field is at its minimum length. When that occurs the data field contains up to 46 characters of information, since pad characters are required to fill the data field to a minimum length of 46 characters. This results in a minimum size Ethernet frame being 72 characters in length.

For a minimum frame length of 72 bytes, the time per frame is 9.6 μs + 72 bytes × 8 bits/byte × 100 ms/bit, or 67.2 × 10^{-6} seconds. Thus, in one second there can be a maximum of 1/67.2 × 10^{-6}, or 14 880 minimum-size 72-byte frames.

Table 6.1 summarizes the frame processing requirements for a 10-Mbps Ethernet network under 50% and 100% load conditions based upon minimum and maximum frame sizes. Note that those frame processing requirements define the frame examination (filtering) operating rate of a bridge connected to an Ethernet. That rate indicates the number of frames per second a bridge connected to a 10-Mbps Ethernet local area network must be capable of examining under heavy (50% load) and full (100% load) traffic conditions. Those frame processing requirements also define the maximum frame forwarding rate for a bridge or router connected to a single network, since if all frames were routed off the network the forwarding rate would equal the filtering rate.

Table 6.1 Ethernet frame processing requirements (frames per second).

Average frame size (bytes)	Frames per second	
	50% load	100% load
1 526	406	812
72	7 440	14 880

Program EPERFORM.BAS

From the two sets of computations previously performed in this section, Ethernet bridge and router processing requirements and 50% and 100% network load conditions were determined. To facilitate performing additional computations, a general model of Ethernet bridge and router processing requirements will be developed which will be incorporated into a BASIC language program. That program, which we will appropriately name EPERFORM.BAS, will be exercised by varying the Ethernet frame size from its minimum frame length of 72 bytes to its maximum frame length of 1526 bytes.

To develop a general model which provides the maximum number of frames that can be transmitted on an Ethernet network, we can simply replace the specific frame length used in prior computations by the variable FLENGTH. Then, we obtain the maximum frame rate in frames per second (FPS) under a 100% network load using the following equation:

Ethernet 100% load frame rate

$$= \frac{1}{9.6 \ \mu s + \text{FLENGTH} \times 8 \ \text{bits/byte} \times 100 \ \text{ns/bit}}$$

Figure 6.2 lists the contents of the program EPERFORM.BAS developed to exercise the previously developed Ethernet frame rate model for frame lengths varying from 72 to 1526 bytes in length under 50% and 100% load conditions. In this program the FOR J loop is used to define four sets of variables for use by the FOR FLENGTH loop which performs the computations required to determine Ethernet frame processing requirements based upon different frame lengths. The first iteration of the J loop simply sets FLENGTH to compute the frame processing requirements for a frame length of 72 bytes. The second iteration of the J loop results in the FLENGTH loop computing the frame processing requirement for frame lengths from 80 to 100 bytes in increments of 20 bytes. The third iteration of the J loop results in the FLENGTH loop computing the frame processing requirements for frame lengths from 125 to 1500 bytes in increments of 25 bytes. Finally, the fourth iteration completes the computations for the maximum frame length of 1526 bytes.

```
REM PROGRAM EPERFORM.BAS
LPRINT "THIS PROGRAM COMPUTES ETHERNET BRIDGE FRAME PROCESSING REQUIREMENTS"
LPRINT "      BASED UPON VARYING AVERAGE ETHERNET FRAME LENGTHS"
LPRINT
LPRINT "AVERAGE FRAME LENGTH       FRAME PROCESSING REQUIREMENT"
LPRINT "                             50% LOAD      100% LOAD"
LPRINT
FOR J = 1 TO 12 STEP 3
READ A, B, C
DATA 72,72,1,80,100,20,125,1500,25,1526,1526,1
FOR FLENGTH = A TO B STEP C
FPS = 1 / (.0000096 + FLENGTH * 8 * .0000001)
LPRINT USING "    #####    "; FLENGTH;
LPRINT USING "              ######.##    ######.##"; FPS / 2; FPS
NEXT FLENGTH
NEXT J
END
```

Figure 6.2 Program listing of EPERFORM.BAS.

Figure 6.3 lists the results obtained from the execution of the program EPERFORM.BAS. By using monitoring equipment, such as a protocol analyzer, you can determine the average frame length transmitted on your network. Then you can use that data in conjunction with the frame processing requirement columns listed in Figure 6.3 to determine the frame processing requirements for your specific network environment. Due to improvements in bridge and router frame processing resulting from the incorporation of low-cost, high-performance microprocessors, such as the Intel 80486, today you should be able to obtain bridges and routers with a processing capability that exceeds the frame processing requirements for all Ethernet frame lengths. Thus, the data listed in Figure 6.3 is primarily of value for deciding whether or not you should continue to use older bridges and routers as your network operation changes.

Another area in which the data presented in Figure 6.3 can be extremely valuable is in evaluating bridges and routers. Suppose you were evaluating two bridges manufactured by the well-known vendors X and Y. Let us assume vendor X's sales literature lists an Ethernet frame processing capability of 15 000 frames per second without specifying the average frame length, while vendor Y's sales literature lists an Ethernet frame processing capability of 20 000 frames per second, also without specifying the average frame length. Which vendor product provides a higher level of capability?

Since each vendor's frame processing rate exceeds 14 880 frames per second, both have the ability to process a fully loaded Ethernet network. Thus, the higher processing capability of vendor Y is irrelevant and you should consider both products to be equivalent with respect to their frame processing capability.

The actual Ethernet operating rate

Now that the maximum number of frames per second that can be carried on a 10-Mbps Ethernet LAN has been determined, that information can be used to determine the utilization of the LAN. To do so we must recognize that the actual number of bits per second that can be carried on a 10-Mbps Ethernet LAN will always be less than 10 Mbps due to the dead time between frames. For example, to compute the actual number of bits transmitted in one second using the maximum length frame, you must subtract the number of bits that cannot be transmitted during the 812 slots of dead time (9.6 μs)

```
THIS PROGRAM COMPUTES ETHERNET BRIDGE FRAME PROCESSING REQUIREMENTS
       BASED UPON VARYING AVERAGE ETHERNET FRAME LENGTHS
```

AVERAGE FRAME LENGTH	FRAME PROCESSING REQUIREMENT	
	50% LOAD	100% LOAD
72	7440.48	14880.95
80	6793.48	13586.96
100	5580.36	11160.71
125	4562.04	9124.09
150	3858.02	7716.05
175	3342.25	6684.49
200	2948.11	5896.23
225	2637.13	5274.26
250	2385.50	4770.99
275	2177.70	4355.40
300	2003.21	4006.41
325	1854.60	3709.20
350	1726.52	3453.04
375	1614.99	3229.97
400	1516.99	3033.98
425	1430.21	2860.41
450	1352.81	2705.63
475	1283.37	2566.74
500	1220.70	2441.41
525	1163.87	2327.75
550	1112.10	2224.20
575	1064.74	2129.47
600	1021.24	2042.48
625	981.16	1962.32
650	944.11	1888.22
675	909.75	1819.51
700	877.81	1755.62
725	848.03	1696.07
750	820.21	1640.42
775	794.16	1588.31
800	769.70	1539.41
825	746.71	1493.43
850	725.06	1450.12
875	704.62	1409.24
900	685.31	1370.61
925	667.02	1334.04
950	649.69	1299.38
975	633.23	1266.46
1000	617.59	1235.18
1025	602.70	1205.40
1050	588.51	1177.02
1075	574.98	1149.95
1100	562.05	1124.10
1125	549.69	1099.38
1150	537.87	1075.73
1175	526.54	1053.07
1200	515.68	1031.35
1225	505.25	1010.51
1250	495.25	990.49
1275	485.63	971.25
1300	476.37	952.74
1325	467.46	934.93
1350	458.88	917.77
1375	450.61	901.23
1400	442.63	885.27
1425	434.93	869.87
1450	427.50	854.99
1475	420.31	840.62
1500	413.36	826.72
1526	406.37	812.74

Figure 6.3 Execution results of program EPERFORM.BAS.

from the LAN operating rate. Then, when 1526-byte frames are transmitted, the actual maximum Ethernet network data transfer operating rate becomes

$$10 \text{ Mbps} - \frac{9.6\mu s}{100 \text{ } ns} \times 812 = 9922\,048 \text{ bps}$$

Thus, for 100% utilization of a 10-Mbps Ethernet when a maximum frame size of 1526 bytes is used, 9.922 Mbps must be transmitted. Since many inexpensive test devices are capable of counting frames, or bits, or both frames and bits, using such equipment with knowledge of the maximum achievable data transfer rate on the network provides us with the ability to compute its utilization. In addition, you may be able to defer the purchase of a more expensive LAN performance analyzer, which, due to the prices of such equipment, may result in a considerable saving.

Network utilization

To illustrate the computations required to determine the level of Ethernet network utilization, let us assume the monitoring of an Ethernet LAN indicates that during 10 minutes of monitoring, a total of 280 000 frames with an average data field length of 100 bytes were counted. The average frame length, including 100 data bytes, would be 126 bytes due to the 26 overhead bytes required to transport each frame. Then the average number of frames per second would be computed as follows:

280 000 frames/10 minutes = 466.67 frames per second

The number of bits per second flowing on the network is computed by multiplying the frame size by 8 bits/byte and then multiplying the result by the frame rate. Thus, 126 bytes/frame × 8 bits/byte × 466.67 frames/second is 470 403 bits per second. Then, the level of utilization would be (470 403/9922 048) × 100%, or 4.74%.

Based upon readily available performance statistics, a 100-node Ethernet can normally be expected to have an average utilization level under 2%, with worst second, minute, and hour utilization levels of 40%, 15–20%, and 3–5%, respectively. These performance statistics represent the activity on a typical Ethernet network in that at any particular time many network users are performing local processing, such as composing a memorandum or electronic message. Other network users may be reading a manual, talking on the telephone, or performing an activity completely unrelated to network usage. Thus, only a few users are actually transmitting or receiving information using the network. Concerning those users, one may be transmitting a short electronic mail message of a few hundred characters, while another might be downloading a file from the server or accessing a server facility. Thus, a typical 2% level of network utilization equates to a data transfer rate of $9922\,048 \times 0.02$, or approximately 198 Kbps. At this data transfer rate many users can be sending electronic messages, interacting with the file server, and performing file transfer operations.

When a number of network users initiate file transfers you can expect a short peak level of utilization to approach or surpass 40%. Since a 640 Kbyte file transfer will require less than 0.7 seconds at 10 Mbps, many file transfers will rapidly be completed, which eliminates the potential for one file transfer to overlap another if two users initiate a file transfer just a second or two apart from one another. This explains why the worst-minute utilization level of an Ethernet network is typically reduced to 15–20% in comparison to a worst second utilization level of 40%. Since our previous computation is much better than the typical worst-minute utilization, it would appear that the monitored LAN is not overloaded. However, an extension of monitoring of several hours of activity during peak periods should be considered to ensure that utilization peaks were not inadvertently missed.

Information transfer rate

Although knowledge concerning the average frame length and frame rate is important, by themselves they do not provide definitive information concerning the rate at which information can be transferred on a network. This is because a portion of an Ethernet frame represents overhead and does not carry actual data. Thus, to obtain a more realistic indication of the ability of an Ethernet network to transfer information you must compute the information transfer rate in bps. This calculation is performed by first subtracting 26 bytes from the frame length for frames with a data field of 46 or more bytes, as there are 26 overhead bytes in each frame. Next, you would multiply the frame rate by the adjusted frame length and then multiply the result by eight to obtain the information transfer rate in bps.

```
CLS
REM PROGRAM EITR.BAS
PRINT "INFORMATION TRANSFER RATE VERSUS AVERAGE FRAME LENGTH"
PRINT
PRINT "AVERAGE FRAME    100% LOAD    INFORMATION TRANSFER"
PRINT "  LENGTH         FRAMES/SEC    RATE IN BPS          "
FOR J = 1 TO 12 STEP 3
READ A, B, C
DATA 72,72,1,80,100,20,125,1500,125,1526,1526,1
FOR FLENGTH = A TO B STEP C
FPS = 1 / (.0000096 + FLENGTH * 8 * .0000001)
PRINT USING "#####          ######"; FLENGTH; FPS;
PRINT USING "          ########"; FPS * (FLENGTH - 26) * 8
NEXT FLENGTH
NEXT J
END
```

Figure 6.4 Program listing of EITR.BAS. This program computes the Ethernet information transfer rate based upon an average frame length and resulting 100% frame rate.

Figure 6.4 lists the statements contained in a program named EITR.BAS. This program was developed to compute the information transfer rate in bps based upon 16 average frame lengths and their corresponding frame transfer rates. Readers will note that the program EITR.BAS represents a simple modification to the previously developed program EPERFORM.BAS. The results of the execution of EITR.BAS are listed in Table 6.2.

In examining the data contained in Table 6.2, let us focus our attention upon the information transfer rate in the third column. Note that at an average frame length of 72 bytes the information transfer rate is approximately 5.48 Mbps, or slightly more than half the Ethernet 10-Mbps operating rate. At an average frame length of 1526 bytes in which all frames are of the maximum length, the information transfer rate increases to approximately 9.75 Mbps. This explains why a large Ethernet network can safely handle many simultaneous file transfer operations without degradation, since a file transfer increases the average frame length which increases the ability of an Ethernet network to transport information.

To visually illustrate how the information transfer rate depends upon the average frame length, the results obtained from the execution of EITR.BAS are plotted as a line graph in Figure 6.5.

Table 6.2 Execution results from program `EITR.BAS`.

Average frame length	100% load frames/second	Information transfer rate (bps)
72	14 881	5 476 191
80	13 587	5 869 565
100	11 161	6 607 143
125	9 124	7 226 278
250	4 771	8 549 618
375	3 230	9 018 088
500	2 441	9 257 812
625	1 962	9 403 454
750	1 640	9 501 312
875	1 409	9 571 590
1 000	1 235	9 624 506
1 125	1 099	9 665 787
1 250	990	9 698 891
1 375	901	9 726 027
1 500	827	9 748 677
1 526	813	9 752 926

Figure 6.5 Frame length vs information transfer rate.

6.2 USING BRIDGES TO ADJUST THE NETWORK

One of the most valuable indicators of poor network response time other than user complaints is a high level of utilization. When Ethernet utilization climbs above 25–35% for long periods of time, either a large number of file transfers are hogging the network or network traffic has grown to the point where you may wish to modify the LAN to increase its performance. One of the most common methods used to improve LAN performance is to split the network into smaller segments through the use of one or more bridges.

Figure 6.6 illustrates the potential use of a local bridge to split an Ethernet into two smaller segments, thereby reducing the traffic on each of the resulting subnets. The maximum number of devices placed on each subnet depends upon the traffic generated by each device, with a higher level of device traffic resulting in a lower limit on the number of devices per segment prior to network performance becoming unacceptable. By using a LAN protocol analyzer, you can obtain an accurate measurement of traffic per device that can assist you in determining both when and where to subdivide the LAN. However, once a decision is made to employ the use of one or more local bridges you should estimate their performance requirements to ensure the equipment you acquire does not become a bottleneck. To do so you should ensure that the filtering and forwarding rate of a bridge under consideration at a minimum exceeds the frame processing rate associated

Figure 6.6 Using a bridge to improve Ethernet LAN performance. By using one or more bridges, a single LAN can be subdivided, reducing the traffic on each of the resulting subnets.

with the average frame length monitored or estimated to be carried on your linked networks. As previously discussed in this chapter, most modern Ethernet bridges fabricated using high performance Intel 80486 microprocessors or similar hardware will provide a level of frame processing which provides the ability to filter and forward frames under 100% loading without becoming a bottleneck.

Predicting throughput

Until now, it was assumed that the operating rate of each LAN linked by a bridge is the same. However, in many organizations, this may not be true due to the implementation of LANs at different times using different technologies. Thus, Accounting could be using a 10-Mbps Ethernet 10BASE-T LAN, while the personnel department might be using an AT&T StarLAN CSMA/CD network operating at 1 Mbps.

Linked LANs

Suppose you wanted to interconnect the two LANs using a local bridge. To predict throughput between LANs, let us use the network configuration illustrated in Figure 6.7. Here the operating rate of LAN A is assumed to be R_1 bps, while the operating rate of LAN B is assumed to be R_2 bps.

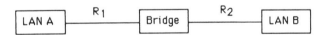

Figure 6.7 Linking LANs with different operating rates. When LANs with different operating rates (R_1 and R_2) are connected via a bridge, access of files across the bridge may result in an unacceptable level of performance.

In one second R_1 bits can be transferred on LAN A and R_2 bits can be transferred on LAN B. Similarly, it takes $1/R_1$ seconds to transfer one bit on LAN A and $1/R_2$ seconds to transfer one bit on LAN B. Thus the time, $1/R_T$, to transfer one bit across the bridge from LAN A to LAN B, ignoring the transfer time at the bridge, is given by

$$\frac{1}{R_T} = \frac{1}{R_1} + \frac{1}{R_2}$$

or

$$R_T = \frac{1}{\frac{1}{R_1} + \frac{1}{R_2}}$$

Previously we computed that a 10-Mbps Ethernet would support a maximum transfer rate of 812 maximum-sized frames per second. If we assume the second LAN, operating at 1 Mbps, is also an Ethernet, we would compute its transfer rate to be approximately 81 maximum-sized frames per second. Thus, the throughput in frames per second would become

$$R_T = \frac{1}{\frac{1}{812} + \frac{1}{81}} = 73 \text{ frames per second}$$

It should be noted that the preceding computation represents a best-case scenario in which it is assumed that one station has full access to the bandwidth of each network as well as to the resources of the bridge. Unfortunately, this is usually the exception rather than the rule, unless some inter-LAN activity is performed at 3 a.m.! Thus, you will want to adjust this frame transfer rate and the key question becomes how to do so. Fortunately, there are a number of low-cost LAN monitoring software products, such as Triticom Corporation's EtherVision and TokenVision software programs, which were described in the author's books *Token-Ring Networks* and *Ethernet Networks*, published by John Wiley & Sons. By using those products you can determine the average number of stations active on a network.

Suppose there were three users on LAN A transmitting data at any given time and two users on LAN B. Then you would adjust the previous computations to reflect the fact that several users share the bandwidth of each linked network. To do so the maximum transfer rate on LAN A would become 812/3, or about 271 frames per second, while the maximum transfer rate on LAN B would become 81/2, or approximately 41 frames per second. Then, the expected throughput which considers the fact that the bandwidth on each network is shared becomes

$$R_T = \frac{1}{\frac{1}{271} + \frac{1}{41}} = 36 \text{ frames per second}$$

Estimating data transfer time

Knowing the transfer rate between LANs can help us answer many common questions as well as provide us with a mechanism for determining whether or not the location of application programs on different servers should be altered. For example, suppose a program was located on a server on LAN B which suddenly became popular for use by workstations on LAN A. If the program required 320 Kbytes of storage, we could estimate the minimum transfer time required to load that program and, depending upon the results of our calculation, we might want to move the program onto a server on LAN A. For this example, the data transfer rate would be 73 frames/second × 1500 bytes/frame, or 109 500 bytes per second. Dividing the data to be transferred by the data transfer rate, we obtain

$$\frac{320 \text{ Kbytes} \times 1024 \text{ bytes/K}}{109\,500 \text{ bytes/second}} = 2.99 \text{ seconds}$$

Similar to our prior notation concerning the computation of the frame rate between linked LANs, the above transfer time computation represents a best-case scenario. That is, it would take 2.99 seconds to transfer the 320 Kbyte file if no other users required the bandwidth of each LAN during the file transfer activity. However, as previously noted, it was assumed that the use of a software monitoring program indicated that three users were actively performing network-related activities on LAN A and two users were performing network-related activities on LAN B. Thus, a more realistic transfer time computation would use a frame rate of 36 frames per second. In modifying our computations, the transfer rate would be 36 frames/second × 1500 bytes/frame, or 54 000 bytes per second. Dividing the data to be transferred by the data transfer rate, we obtain

$$\frac{320 \text{ Kbytes} \times 1024 \text{ bytes/K}}{54\,000 \text{ bytes/second}} = 6.07 \text{ seconds}$$

Here, the 6.07 seconds represents the average transfer time between networks, while the 2.99 seconds transfer time represents the optimum transfer time.

Considering remote connections

We can extend our analysis of Ethernet frames and the process by which we can estimate data transfer time by considering the frame rate supported by different link speeds. For example, let us consider a pair of remote bridges connected by a 9.6-Kbps line. The time per frame for a 72-byte frame at 9.6 Kbps is $9.6 \times 10^{-6} + 72 \times 8 \times 0.000\ 104\ 1$ seconds/bit, or 0.059 9712 seconds per frame. Thus, in one second the number of frames is 1/0.059 9712, or 16.67 frames per second. Table 6.3 compares the frame per second rate supported by different link speeds for minimum and maximum size Ethernet frames. As expected, the frame transmission rate supported by a 10-Mbps link for minimum and maximum size frames is exactly the same as the frame processing requirements under 100% loading as previously indicated in Table 6.1.

In examining Table 6.3 readers should note that the entries in this table do not consider the effect of the overhead of a protocol used to transport frames between two networks. Thus, readers should decrease the frame per second rate by approximately 20% for all link speeds through 1.536 Mbps. The reason why the 10-Mbps rate should not be adjusted is that it represents a local bridge connection that does not require the use of a wide area network protocol to transport frames. Readers should also note that the link speed of 1.536 Mbps represents a T1 transmission facility that operates at 1.544 Mbps. However, since the framing bits on a T1 circuit use 8 Kbps, the effective line speed available for the transmission of data is 1.536 Mbps.

Table 6.3 Link speed vs frame rate.

| Link speed | Frames per second | |
	Minimum	Maximum
9.6 Kbps	16.67	0.79
19.2 Kbps	33.38	1.58
56.0 Kbps	97.44	4.60
64.0 Kbps	111.17	5.25
1.536 Mbps	2 815.31	136.34
10 Mbps	14 880	812

Once you determine the frame transfer rate supported by a remote connection you can use a precise value based upon knowledge of the average frame rate monitored or estimated to be carried by the network only if that rate falls between the frame rate range noted in Table 6.3. Otherwise, you would use the range of frame rates listed in Table 6.3 in your computations to obtain a range of transfer times. For example, assume you wish to link two LANs using remote bridges as illustrated in Figure 6.8a. If the DSUs operate at 56 Kbps they are able to support a frame transmission rate between 4.6 and 97.44 frames per second prior to adjusting the rate downward by 20% to account for the wide area network protocol overhead. If you monitored LAN A and determined the average frame rate to be 250 frames per second, you could not use that value as the potential frame rate between LANs as it would exceed the transmission capacity of the circuit. Without prior knowledge obtained from monitoring the circuit you would also use the range of frame rates listed in Table 6.3 and adjust them downward by 20% to account for the wide area network protocol overhead. For either situation you would then estimate the data transfer time between stations on one network from that on another by considering the operating rate of each network and the remote connection. Figure 6.8b illustrates the operating rate components for the network topology shown in Figure 6.8a.

A. Topology

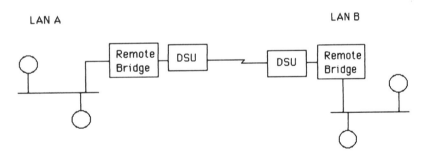

B. Operating rate model components

Legend: DSU = digital service unit

Figure 6.8 Linking remote networks.

To determine the frame transfer rate between remotely connected networks you would then solve the following equation:

$$\frac{1}{R_T} = \frac{1}{R1} + \frac{1}{R_2} + \frac{1}{R_3}$$

Solving for R_T, we obtain

$$R_T = \frac{R_1 R_2 R_3}{R_2 R_3 + R_1 R_3 + R_2 R_3}$$

By using specific values for R_1, R_2, and R_3 we would determine R_T, which would provide us with the frame transfer rate between networks. Then, knowing the file size and average frame rate you could compute the transfer time in the same manner as previously computed.

As indicated in this chapter, you can use your knowledge of the structure and operation of Ethernet LANs to compute a number of performance measurements. Some of those measurements provide you with a basis for selecting an appropriately performing bridge or router, while other calculations provide you with the ability to estimate the time required to load programs across a bridge connecting LANs operating at different data rates. These calculations also provide you with the tools necessary to adjust the configuration of LANs and recognize requirements to move application programs to different servers to increase network performance.

ESTIMATING TOKEN-RING NETWORK PERFORMANCE

In Chapter 6 our attention was focused upon Ethernet network performance and we developed a mathematical model to determine the frame rate based upon different frame lengths. The results of that model were then used to determine the information transfer capability of a 10-Mbps Ethernet network based upon different frame sizes. As you might intuitively expect, the use of larger frames provided a higher information transfer capability since each Ethernet frame is separated from preceding and succeeding frames by a uniform time gap. Thus, longer frames were expected to be more efficient and this was determined to be true.

In this chapter our attention will turn to Token-Ring network performance in a similar manner to our method of examining Ethernet performance. That is, we will first develop a model which is representative of the flow of data on a Token-Ring network. Then, we will exercise the model both manually as well as through the use of a BASIC language program to determine the frame rate as a function of the number of stations on the network and the ring length as well as several other variables. In doing so we will note that the performance models for CSMA/CD and Token-Ring networks considerably differ due to the basic differences between each network access protocol.

In a CSMA/CD network the transmission of a frame is read by all stations without one station's reading activity delaying another station's reading activity. In a Token-Ring network the opposite is true, since station n must process a token or frame prior to passing it onto station $n + 1$ on the network. Thus, the Token-Ring model that will be developed in this chapter will considerably differ from the previously developed Ethernet model presented in Chapter 6. A second area of difference concerns the cabling structure of Ethernet and Token-Ring networks. Most Ethernet bus-based networks use a fraction of the cabling used in the star-bus topology of a Token-Ring. Thus, propagation delay time assumes a much more meaningful role in determining network performance, and results in the inclusion of the speed in which tokens and frames traverse the cable in the Token-Ring model that we will develop in this chapter.

7.1 TOKEN-RING TRAFFIC MODELING

In comparison to Ethernet the modeling of a Token-Ring network can be much more complex. This is because the frame rate depends upon the number of nodes in a network, the token holding time per node, the type of wire used for cabling and ring length, and the type of adapter used as a ring interface unit.

The number of nodes and their cabling govern both token propagation time and holding time as a token flows around the ring. The type of adapter used governs the maximum frame rate supported. This rate can vary between vendors as well as within a vendor's product line. For example, Texas Instruments' original MAC code permitted a maximum transmission of 2200 64 Kbyte frames per second. New software from that vendor raised the frame rate to 3300 and a more recent release known as Turbo MAC 2.1 increased it to 4000 frames per second.

The type of cabling and ring length govern the propagation delay associated with the flow of tokens and frames around the ring. Although the data rate around a ring is consistent at either 4 Mbps or 16 Mbps, tokens and frames do not flow instantaneously around the ring and are delayed, depending upon the distance they must traverse and the type of cabling used. In addition, a slight delay is encountered at each node since the token must be examined to determine its status.

Model development

In developing a model to determine Token-Ring frame rates let us assume there are N stations on the network. Then, on the average a token will travel $N/2$ stations until it is grabbed and converted into a frame. Similarly, a frame can be expected to travel $N/2$ stations until it reaches its destination and another $N/2$ stations until it returns to the origination station and is reconverted back into a token.

As mentioned at the beginning of this chapter, performance of a Token-Ring network is typically more dependent upon the total network cable length than that of an Ethernet network. Thus, in developing a model of Token-Ring network performance a mechanism is required to equate cable length to the propagation delay of electrons flowing on the cable. To do so let us start with the well-known velocity of light.

Propagation delay

In free space the velocity of light is 186 000 miles per second. In a twisted pair cable the speed of electrons is approximately 62% of the velocity of light in free space. Thus, electrons will travel at approximately $186\,000 \times 0.62$, or 115 320 miles per second. Since there are 5280 feet in a mile, this rate is equivalent to 608 889 600 feet per second or approximately 609 feet per microsecond. Then to traverse 1000 feet of cable would require $1000/609 \times 10^6$, or approximately 1.64×10^{-6} seconds.

At a Token-Ring operating rate of 4 Mbps, the bit duration is $1/4000\,000$, or 2.5×10^{-7} seconds. At a network operating rate of 16 Mbps, the bit duration is $1/16\,000\,000$, or 0.625×10^{-7} seconds. Since the time required for electrons to traverse 1000 feet of cable is 1.64×10^{-6} seconds, the cable propagation delay time per 1000 feet of cable can be converted into a bit time delay to simplify computations. At a Token-Ring operating rate of 4 Mbps the bit time delay per 1000 feet of cable becomes $1.64 \times 10^{-6}/2.5 \times 10^{-7}$, or 6.56 bit times. When the Token-Ring network operates at 16 Mbps the bit time delay per 1000 feet of cable becomes $1.64 \times 10^{-6}/0.625 \times 10^{-7}$, or 26.24 bit times.

4-Mbps model

In developing a Token-Ring performance model, let us commence our effort by assuming that the network operates at 4 Mbps. Once we develop this model and use it to perform a series of manual calculations, we will then construct a general model applicable to both 4- and 16-Mbps networks. That model will then be used as a basis for developing a BASIC language program that will be used to generate a comprehensive series of tables contained in Appendix B, as well as two tables in this chapter whose entries we will examine in detail. The tables contained in Appendix B can be used to facilitate determining the frame flow on a Token-Ring network since they enable the frame flow computations to be supplemented by a table lookup process. The tables in this chapter can be considered to represent extracts from Appendix B and their use serves as a guide to the use of the tables contained in Appendix B.

For the development of a 4-Mbps Token-Ring performance model let us start with the flow of a token as indicated by the following steps in the model development process.

1. Given a Token-Ring network with N stations, a free token travels on the average $N/2$ stations until it is grabbed and converted into a frame.

2. Each station adds a 2.5-bit time delay to examine the token. At a 4-Mbps ring operating rate a bit time equals 2.5×10^{-7} seconds. Thus, each station induces a delay of $2.5 \times 2.5 \times 10^{-7}$, or 6.25×10^{-7} seconds.

3. The token consists of three bytes or 24 bits. The time required for the token to be placed onto the ring is

$$24 \times 2.5 \times 10^{-7} \text{ seconds/bit} = 60 \times 10^{-7} \text{ seconds}$$

4. The time for the token to be placed onto the ring and to flow around half the ring until it is grabbed is the sum of the times of step 2 and step 3. This time then becomes

$$N/2 \times 6.25 \times 10^{-7} + 60 \times 10^{-7}$$

5. Once a token is grabbed it is converted into a frame. On the average the frame will travel $N/2$ stations to its destination. A frame containing 64 bytes of information consists of 85 bytes, since 21 bytes of overhead, including starting and ending delimiters, source and destination addresses, and other control information, must be included in the frame. Thus, the time required to place the frame on the ring becomes

$$85 \text{ bytes} \times 8 \text{ bits/byte} \times 2.5 \times 10^{-7} \text{ seconds/bit} = 1.7 \times 10^{-4} \text{ seconds}$$

6. If the network contains N stations the frame must traverse

$N/2$ stations on the average to reach its destination. Thus, the time required for the frame to be placed onto the ring and to traverse half the ring becomes

$$1.7 \times 10^{-4} + N/2 \times 6.25 \times 10^{-7} \text{ seconds}$$

7. The total token and frame time from steps 4 and 6 above is

$$N/2 \times 6.25 \times 10^{-7} + 60 \times 10^{-7} + N/2 \times 6.25 \times 10^{-7} + 1.7 \times 10^{-4}$$
$$\text{or } N \times 6.25 \times 10^{-7} + 60 \times 10^{-7} + 1.7 \times 10^{-4} \text{ seconds}$$

8. Once the frame reaches its destination it must traverse another $N/2$ stations on the average to return to its originating station which then removes it from the network. When this occurs the originating station generates a new token onto the network and the previously described process is repeated. The time for the frame to again traverse half of the network becomes

$$N/2 \times 6.25 \times 10^{-7} \text{ seconds}$$

This time must be added to the time in step 7. Doing so we obtain

$$N \times 9.375 \times 10^{-7} + 60 \times 10^{-7} + 1.7 \times 10^{-4} \text{ seconds}$$

9. To consider the effect of propagation delay time as tokens and frames flow in the cable we must consider the sum of the ring length and twice the sum of all lobe distances. Here we must double the lobe distances since the token will flow to and from each workstation on the lobe. If we let C equal the number of thousands of feet of cable, we obtain the time in seconds to traverse the ring as

$$N \times 9.375 \times 10^{-7} + 60 \times 10^{-7} + 1.7 \times 10^{-4} + 1.64 \times 10^{-6} \times C$$

which equals

$$N \times 9.375 \times 10^{-7} + 1.76 \times 10^{-4} + 1.64 \times 10^{-6} \times C$$

where:

N = number of stations
C = thousands of feet of cable

Exercising the model

To illustrate the use of the above Token-Ring performance model, let us assume a Token-Ring network of 50 stations has 8000 feet of cable. Then, with $N = 50$ and $C = 8$, the time for a token and frame to circulate the ring becomes

$$50 \times 9.375 \times 10^{-7} + 1.76 \times 10^{-4} + 1.64 \times 10^{-6} \times 8$$
$$= 468.75 \times 10^{-7} + 1.76 \times 10^{-4} + 13.12 \times 10^{-6}$$
$$= 0.46875 \times 10^{-4} + 1.76 \times 10^{-4} + 0.1312 \times 10^{-4}$$
$$= 2.36 \times 10^{-4} \text{ seconds}$$

Thus, in one second there will be on the average $1/2.36 \times 10^{-4}$, or 4237, 64-byte information frames that can flow on a Token-Ring network containing 50 stations and a total of 8000 feet of cable.

Network modification

To illustrate the use of the previously developed model in determining the effect of cabling and network stations upon the frame rate, let us now consider what happens when the network is reduced in size. Suppose the number of workstations is halved to 25 and the total cable distance reduced to 4000 feet. Then, with $N = 25$ and $C = 4$, the time for a token and frame to flow around the ring becomes

$$25 \times 9.375 \times 10^{-7} + 1.76 \times 10^{-4} + 1.64 \times 10^{-6} \times 4$$
$$= 0.234375 \times 10^{-4} + 1.76 \times 10^{-4} + 0.0656 \times 10^{-4}$$
$$= 2.06 \times 10^{-4} \text{ seconds}$$

Thus, in one second there will be on the average $1/2.06 \times 10^{-4}$, or 4854, 64-byte information frames. As we would intuitively expect, as the number of stations and cable distance decrease the transmission capacity of the ring increases.

Varying the frame size

Now let us examine the effect of transmitting larger information frames. Suppose we transmit 4000-byte information frames.

Here a total of 4021 bytes is required. Thus, the time required for the frame to be placed on the ring becomes

$$4021 \times 8 \times 2.5 \times 10^{-7} = 80.42 \times 10^{-4} \text{ seconds}$$

Then, the total token and frame time becomes

$$N \times 9.375 \times 10^{-7} + 60 \times 10^{-7} + 80.42 \times 10^{-4} + 1.64 \times 10^{-6} \times C$$

Again, let us assume the number of stations, N, is 50, while the cabling distance is 8000 feet. Thus, we obtain the token and frame revolution time as follows:

$$50 \times 9.375 \times 10^{-7} + 60 \times 10^{-7} + 80.42 \times 10^{-4} + 1.6 \times 10^{-6} \times 8$$
$$= 0.46875 \times 10^{-4} + 0.06 \times 10^{-4} + 80.42 \times 10^{-4} + 0.1312 \times 10^{-4}$$
$$= 81.08 \times 10^{-4} \text{ seconds}$$

Thus, in one second there will be $1/81.08 \times 10^{-4}$ or 123.3 frames. Since each frame contains 4000 bytes of information, the effective operating rate becomes $123.3 \times 4000 \times 8$, or 3.946 Mbps for a 50-station Token-Ring network with 8000 feet of cable using 4000-character information frames. In comparison, a similar Token-Ring network using 64-byte information frames would have a frame rate of 4237 frames per second. However, this rate would be equivalent to an information transfer rate of $4237 \times 64 \times 8$, or 2.169 Mbps. Thus, larger frame sizes provide a more efficient data transportation capability.

The preceding computations which represent the use of a simplified model of a 4-Mbps Token-Ring network, indicate an important concept. That is, the frame length, cabling distance, and number of network stations govern the maximum frame rate that can flow on a Token-Ring network. This tells us that when a network becomes saturated due to heavy usage you should consider breaking larger networks into subnetworks interconnected by bridges to improve Token-Ring network performance. The model presented above is simplified due to the fact that it does not include the effect of the flow of network management frames which, when they flow on the network, preclude the transfer of data. For example, every seven seconds the active monitor transmits an Active Monitor Present frame for which all other stations respond with a Standby Monitor Present frame. Since the frame rate on a Token-Ring network will range from over 100 frames per second when the frame length approaches the maximum-size frame length on a 4-Mbps network, to many thousands of frames per second when the minimum-length frame is transmitted, the effect of the Active Monitor Present frames and responding Standby Monitor Present frame every seven seconds is negligible upon network performance. This is because those two frames are relatively short and would result in a maximum of 260 frames every seven seconds during which approximately 15 000 or more similar length frames could be transported on the network. Thus, the use of a simplified model does not materially affect our model.

Adapter card considerations

One of the more interesting aspects of Token-Ring frame rates is that the majority of adapter cards from different vendors which use the Texas Instrument chip set support a maximum frame rate of 4000 frames per second. This indicates that a further constraint to the number of nodes and cable length is the adapter cards used in a network. In 1991 Madge Systems introduced an adapter card which was capable of transmitting approximately 12 000 64-byte frames per second. Thus, using that firm's adapter card or other higher performance adapter cards manufactured by other vendors can significantly improve the performance of a Token-Ring network. However, the use of such high performance adapter cards is irrelevant when a network grows in size in terms of the number of network stations and cable distance. In such situations the capability of high performance network adapter cards cannot be effectively used.

Now that we have developed and exercised a mathematical model to determine the frame rate on a 4-Mbps Token-Ring network, we will use our prior effort to develop a general model for 4- and 16-Mbps networks. In doing so let us use BASIC language variables so that we can exercise our model through its incorporation into a BASIC language program.

General model development

To denote the difference between 4- and 16-Mbps networks, let us use the array variable BITTIME(I). Then, we can assign the value 1/4000 000 to BITTIME(1) to represent the bit time duration on a 4-Mbps Token-Ring network and the value

1/16 000 000 to BITTIME(2) to represent the bit time duration on a 16-Mbps network.

Referring to our previous nine-step approach used in the development of a 4-Mbps Token-Ring performance model, step 2 computed the station delay. Using the variable S.DELAY to represent the station delay, we obtain

$$S.DELAY = 2.5 * BITTIME(I)$$

In step 3 we determined the time to place a token on the ring. Using the variable T.PLACEMENT to represent the token placement time, we obtain

$$T.PLACEMENT = 24 * BITTIME(I)$$

Then, using the variable H.TRINGFLOW to represent the time for a token to be placed on the network and traverse half the ring (step 4 in our earlier model), we obtain

$$H.TRINGFLOW = (N/2) * S.DELAY + T.PLACEMENT$$

Once a token is grabbed it is converted into a frame. Since the time required to place the frame onto the ring depends upon the length of the frame, let us use the array variable FRAMELENGTH(F) to denote different frame lengths. In actuality, let us assign different information field values to each FRAMELENGTH(F) value and add 21 bytes to represent the overhead per frame. Then, if we use the variable FRAMETIME to denote the time required to place a frame on the ring, we obtain

$$FRAMETIME = (FRAMELENGTH(F) + 21) * 8 * BITTIME(I)$$

As noted in step 6 in our prior model, the frame must traverse $N/2$ stations on the average to reach its destination. If we denote the variable H.FRAMEFLOW to represent the time required for the frame to be placed on the ring and flow $N/2$ stations down the ring, we obtain

$$H.FRAMEFLOW = (N/2) * S.DELAY + FRAMETIME$$

If we use the variable C to denote the cable length (ring plus twice each lobe distance) in 1000-foot increments and the variable C.PROPTIME to denote the propagation delay time, we obtain

$$C.PROPTIME = C * 1.64E - 06$$

Then to compute the frame rate using the variable FPS, we obtain

$$FPS = 1/(TOTAL.TIME + C.PROPTIME)$$

Program TPERFORM.BAS

To facilitate the execution of our general Token-Ring performance model, the program TPERFORM.BAS was developed. This program, whose statements are listed in Figure 7.1, can be used to generate a series of tables which indicates the frame rate based upon the network operating rate, number of stations on the network, average frame length, and network cable length in 1000-foot increments. As previously noted, the frame length is specified in terms of the information field to which 21 bytes representing frame overhead are added.

In examining the program listing of TPERFORM.BAS note that the FOR--NEXT loops which vary the number of stations, frame length, and cable length would result in 910 frame rate computations for each ring operating rate. Rather than place a large set of tables in this chapter, the results obtained from the execution of TPERFORM.BAS are placed in Appendix B. In addition, readers can modify the entries in the DATA statement to initialize a specific frame length more applicable to their network or change the FOR--NEXT loop variable values for N and/or C to obtain information concerning the frame rate for a specific number of stations or cable length that is not included in Appendix B.

To provide readers with an example of the ease with which TPERFORM.BAS can be modified as well as data we can use to further discuss Token-Ring performance, let us modify the program. By changing the FOR N loop parameters to 40 TO 50 STEP 5 and the FOR F loop parameters to 1 TO 2 STEP 1, the printed output contained in Tables 7.1 and 7.2 is obtained.

General observations

In reviewing the results of the frame rate computations presented in Table 7.1, let us first examine the effect of a change in the average frame length compared with a change in the cable length of a network. This will enable us to determine the relative effects of average frame length and cable distance for a

```
REM PROGRAM TPERFORM.BAS
       CLS
REM THIS PROGRAM GENERATES A SERIES OF TABLES INDICATING THE FRAME RATE
REM ON A TOKEN-RING NETWORK BASED UPON THE NETWORK OPERATING RATE, NUMBER
REM OF STATIONS, AVERAGE FRAME LENGTH AND TOTAL NETWORK CABLE LENGTH
          FOR K = 1 TO 7                       ' initialize frame lenghts
          READ FRAMELENGTH(K)
          NEXT K
          DATA 64,128,256,512,1024,2048,4096
          BITTIME(1) = 1 / 4000000             ' initialize bit duration
          BITTIME(2) = 1 / 16000000
          RATE$(1) = "4MBPS"                    ' initialize network rate
          RATE$(2) = "16MBPS"
START:

          LCOUNT = 0                            ' initialize line count
          FOR I = 1 TO 2                        ' vary network operating rate
          IF I = 1 THEN GOTO NXT
          FOR LC = 1 TO 50 - LCOUNT: LPRINT : NEXT LC: LCOUNT = 0
NXT:      GOSUB HOUTPT                          ' print page header
          FOR N = 10 TO 260 STEP 10             ' vary number of stations
          FOR F = 1 TO 7 STEP 1                 ' vary frame length (bytes)
          FOR C = 2 TO 10 STEP 2                ' vary cable length (per 1000 feet)
          S.DELAY = 2.5 * BITTIME(I)
          T.PLACEMENT = 24 * BITTIME(I)
          H.TRINGFLOW = (N / 2) * S.DELAY + T.PLACEMENT
          FRAMETIME = (FRAMELENGTH(F) + 21) * 8 * BITTIME(I)
          H.FRAMEFLOW = (N / 2) * S.DELAY + FRAMETIME
          TOTAL.TIME = H.TRINGFLOW + H.FRAMEFLOW + (N / 2) * S.DELAY
          C.PROPTIME = C * .00000164#
          FPS = 1 / (TOTAL.TIME + C.PROPTIME)
          GOSUB DOUTPT
          NEXT C
          NEXT F
          NEXT N
          NEXT I
          END
HOUTPT:
          LPRINT "FRAME RATE OF A "; RATE$(I); " TOKEN-RING NETWORK"
          LPRINT "BASED UPON THE NETWORK OPERATING RATE, NUMBER OF"
          LPRINT "STATIONS, FRAME LENGTH AND TOTAL CABLE LENGTH "
          LPRINT
          LPRINT "NUMBER OF  AVG FRAME    CABLE LENGTH   FRAME RATE"
          LPRINT "STATIONS    LENGTH       X000 FEET      IN FPS"
          RETURN
DOUTPT:
          IF LCOUNT < 50 THEN GOTO SKIP
          FOR LC = 1 TO 10                      ' move to top of next page
          LPRINT
          NEXT LC
          LCOUNT = 0
          GOSUB HOUTPT
SKIP:     LPRINT USING "  ####     ######"; N; FRAMELENGTH(F);
          LPRINT USING "          ###"; C;
          LPRINT USING "        ######## "; FPS
          LCOUNT = LCOUNT + 1
          RETURN
```

Figure 7.1 Program listing of TPERFORM.BAS.

Table 7.1 Frame rate of a 4-Mbps Token-Ring network based upon the network operating rate, number of stations, frame length, and total cable length.

Number of stations	Avg frame length	Cable length ×000 feet	Frame rate in FPS
40	64	2	4613
40	64	4	4544
40	64	6	4477
40	64	8	4413
40	64	10	4350
40	128	2	2900
40	128	4	2873
40	128	6	2846
40	128	8	2820
40	128	10	2794
45	64	2	4515
45	64	4	4449
45	64	6	4385
45	64	8	4323
45	64	10	4263
45	128	2	2861
45	128	4	2835
45	128	6	2809
45	128	8	2783
45	128	10	2758
50	64	2	4422
50	64	4	4359
50	64	6	4297
50	64	8	4237
50	64	10	4179
50	128	2	2824
50	128	4	2798
50	128	6	2772
50	128	8	2747
50	128	10	2723

network with a given number of stations. Next, we will observe the effect on the frame rate of an increase in the number of network stations.

For a 40-station network with an average frame length of 64 bytes, note that each increase in network cabling by 2000 feet results in a decrease in the frame rate ranging from 69 (4613 – 4544) to 63 (4413 – 4350) frames per second. Note that a 40-station network with an average frame length of 128 bytes has a

Table 7.2 Frame rate of a 16-Mbps Token-Ring network based upon the network operating rate, number of stations, frame length, and total cable length.

Number of stations	Avg frame length	Cable length ×000 feet	Frame rate in FPS
40	64	2	17651
40	64	4	16685
40	64	6	15819
40	64	8	15039
40	64	10	14332
40	128	2	11280
40	128	4	10877
40	128	6	10503
40	128	8	10153
40	128	10	9826
45	64	2	17293
45	64	4	16365
45	64	6	15531
45	64	8	14778
45	64	10	14095
45	128	2	11133
45	128	4	10740
45	128	6	10375
45	128	8	10033
45	128	10	9714
50	64	2	16950
50	64	4	16057
50	64	6	15253
50	64	8	14527
50	64	10	13866
50	128	2	10989
50	128	4	10607
50	128	6	10250
50	128	8	9917
50	128	10	9604

decrease in the frame rate ranging from 27 (2900 − 2873) to 26 (2820 − 2794) frames per second as the cable length increases in 2000-foot increments from 2000 to 10 000 feet. When the average frame length is 64 bytes, a decrease in frame flow of 64 frames per second per 2000-foot cable length increase is equivalent to a decrease of 64 × 64 × 8, or 32 768 bits per second in the information flow capability of the network. When the average frame length is 128 bytes, a decrease in frame flow of 26 frames per second due to a cable length increase of 2000 feet results in a decrease of $128 \times 26 \times 8$, or 26 624 bits per second in the flow of information. Thus, as the average frame length increases, the effect of an increase in the amount of cabling used in the network slightly decreases.

Now let us examine the frame rate as the average frame length increases and the number of stations remains fixed. Note that for a 40-station network, an increase in the average frame rate from 64 to 128 bytes for a cable length of 2000 feet results in a decrease in the frame rate of 1713 (4613 − 2900) frames per second. For a cable length of 10 000 feet, an increase in the average frame length from 64 to 128 bytes for a 40-station network results in a decrease in the frame rate of 1556 (4350 − 2794) frames per second. Thus, the effect of the frame length upon the frame rate exceeds the effect of the cable length.

Now let us turn our attention to observing the effect of an increase in the number of network stations with a fixed average frame length and cable length. For a 40-station network that has an average frame length of 64 bytes and a cable length of 2000 feet, the frame rate is 4613 frames per second. When the number of stations is increased to 45 the frame rate drops to 4515—a decrease of almost 100 frames per second. On a per-station-increase basis, this results in a decrease of approximately 20 frames per second when the average frame length is 64 bytes. Note that this decrease in the frame rate is slightly less than the decrease in the frame rate as the network cable distance increases in 800-foot steps from 2000 to 10 000 feet. This means that each increase in the number of stations has a lesser effect upon network performance than an increase of 800 feet in the cabling used in a network. Although these figures slightly differ as the number of stations on a network increases, you can use the preceding as a general guide for configuring and expanding Token-Ring networks. That is, by limiting your network cabling distance you may be able to alleviate the effect of an increase in the number of network stations on network performance.

Station effect upon network performance

To obtain a more detailed understanding of the effect of an increase in the number of network stations upon network performance, the comprehensive series of tables contained in

Appendix B was used to extract data. In doing so the frame rate for 4- and 16-Mbps Token-Ring networks was extracted for 64-byte frame lengths and 10 000 feet of cable as the number of network stations varied from 10 to 260 in increments of 10 stations. Table 7.3 contains the frame rate information extracted from Appendix B.

In examining the frame rates for 4- and 16-Mbps networks listed in Table 7.3, note that the number of stations has a considerable effect upon the information flow on a Token-Ring network. For example, a 10-station 4-Mbps network supports

Table 7.3 Frame rate vs number of network stations (based upon a 64-byte average frame length and 10 000 feet of network cabling).

Number of stations	Frames per second	
	4 Mbps	16 Mbps
10	4 956	15 938
20	4 736	15 364
30	4 535	14 830
40	4 350	14 332
50	4 179	13 866
60	4 022	13 430
70	3 876	13 020
80	3 740	12 634
90	3 613	12 271
100	3 495	11 928
110	3 384	11 603
120	3 280	11 296
130	3 182	11 005
140	3 090	10 728
150	3 003	10 465
160	2 921	10 215
170	2 843	9 976
180	2 769	9 748
190	2 699	9 530
200	2 632	9 322
210	2 569	9 123
220	2 508	8 932
230	2 451	8 748
240	2 396	8 573
250	2 343	8 404
260	2 293	8 241

a frame rate of 4956 frames per second, which is equivalent to an information transfer rate of 4956 frames/second × 64 bytes/frame × 8 bits/byte, or 2.537 Mbps. For a 260-station network, the frame rate is reduced to 2293 frames per second, which is equivalent to an information transfer rate of 2293 frames/second × 64 bytes/frame × 8 bits/byte, or 1.174 Mbps. Turning our attention to the frame rates listed in Table 7.3 for a 16-Mbps Token-Ring, note that a 10-station network supports an information flow of 15 938 frames/second × 64 bytes/frame × 8 bits/byte, or 8.16 Mbps. When the number of stations is increased to 260, the information rate decreases to 8241 frames/second × 64 bytes/frame × 8 bits/byte, or 4.219 Mbps. Although the primary reason why a Token-Ring network supports a maximum of 260 network stations is based upon 'jitter' of the bits flowing on the network, the approximate halving of the information transfer capability is another important consideration for limiting the number of stations on a network.

7.2 BRIDGE AND ROUTER PERFORMANCE REQUIREMENTS

In the first section in this chapter we focused our attention upon the development of mathematical models to estimate the flow of data on 4- and 16-Mbps Token-Ring networks. In this section we will use our previously obtained knowledge about Token-Ring performance to examine the flow of data between networks when bridges are used. In doing so we will obtain answers to such questions as 'What is the forwarding and filtering rate required to be supported by a Token-Ring bridge or router prior to that device becoming a potential internet bottleneck?' and 'What effect does the use of different types of wide area network transmission facilities have upon the data transfer capability of Token-Ring remote bridges and routers?'. Since the use of wide area network transmission facilities is only applicable to remote bridges and routers, let us first examine the required level of performance of a local bridge and then turn our attention to the use of remote bridges and routers.

Local bridges

Figure 7.2 illustrates the use of a local bridge to connect two Token-Ring networks. Here, each Token-Ring network can

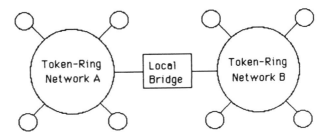

Figure 7.2 Using a local Token-Ring bridge. The performance required by a local Token-Ring bridge is primarily dependent upon the operating rate of each network to be connected, the number of stations on each network, the average frame length on each network, and the total length of cabling used on each network.

operate at either 4 or 16 Mbps, resulting in three distinct mixtures of network operating speeds the bridge must support—4 and 4 Mbps, 4 and 16 Mbps, and 16 and 16 Mbps. Thus, the level of performance required by a local bridge linking Token-Ring networks will depend upon the average frame length, the total cable length, the number of stations, and the operating rate of each network. Obtaining this information will provide you with the frame rate in frames per second that you can expect each network to carry. Then, the frame processing capability of the local bridge should equal the sum of the frame rate expected to be carried by each Token-Ring network or the bridge will become a network bottleneck.

Considering a performance range

Since the average frame length carried on a network varies with time and the number of stations on a network expands and contracts in tandem with personnel changes and corporate policy, instead of determining one number you may prefer to work with a range of values. As an alternative, you may wish to select a network situation in which a bridge meeting the frame rate requirements of a certain networking scenario can be expected to satisfy a large variance in future changes to each Token-Ring network to be interconnected. For example, assume you have a 4-Mbps and a 16-Mbps Token-Ring network you wish to locally connect, and through monitoring you have determined that the average frame length on each network was 128 bytes. Assuming the 4-Mbps network has 50 stations and the 16-Mbps network has 80 stations and each network uses

6000 feet of cable, you would use Appendix B to determine that the expected frame rate on the 4-Mbps network is 2772 fps while the expected frame rate on the 16-Mbps network is 9561 fps. Then, the local bridge should have a frame filtering capability equal to the sum of each network expected frame rate, or 12 333 fps. However, what happens if either network changes?

Considering the effect of network changes

If the number of stations and length of network cabling increases, the frame rate on the network decreases. Thus, an increase in either or both of those variables has no effect upon a bridge acquired to support the frame rate of smaller networks. Similarly, an increase in the average frame length results in a decrease in the frame rate on each network. Since the most variable factor is the average frame length, you may wish to consider selecting a lower average frame length which in effect increases the network frame rate. In doing so you are adding a margin of safety to the processing requirements of a local Token-Ring bridge. For example, lowering the average frame length to 64 bytes while keeping the number of stations and cable length of the network constant results in the 4-Mbps network being projected to have a frame rate of 4297 fps, while the 16-Mbps network has its frame rate projection increased to 13 776 fps. Then, the local bridge you would use to connect the two networks should have the capability to process 18 073 64-byte frames per second. Concerning the bridge forwarding rate, under a worst case scenario assume each frame on each network for a short period of time is routed to the other network. Then, the forwarding rate of the local bridge should equal its filtering rate to ensure that the bridge will not become a network bottleneck and cannot congest the flow of data between networks.

Remote bridges and routers

As previously noted, the performance requirement for a local bridge is simply the sum of the frame rate on each connected network. That aggregate number of frames per second provides you with the overall frame processing rate a local bridge must exceed prior to it becoming a potential network bottleneck. In turning our attention to remote bridges and routers used to connect two geographically dispersed Token-Ring networks, we must consider the operating rate of the wide area network transmission facility used to connect networks. Unless that transmission facility operates at the network operating rate, a condition which essentially occurs only when a local bridge is used, the transmission facility functions as a filter which reduces the maximum potential forwarding rate of frames routed from one network to the other network.

Wide area network operating rate

There are three key variables which govern the frame rate that can be achieved on a wide area transmission facility used to interconnect remotely located Token-Ring networks. Those variables include the frame lengths, the WAN operating rate, and the overhead of the transmission protocol used to transport frames between networks. Since the protocol overhead can vary, depending upon the type of protocol used by a bridge or router manufacturer as well as by their use of data compression, we will first examine the maximum frame rate for different frame lengths without considering the effect of the protocol or presence or absence of data compression.

Program TRWAN.BAS

To facilitate the computation of frame rates for different average frame lengths the BASIC language program TRWAN.BAS was developed. Figure 7.3 lists the statements in that program which computes the frame rate for average frame lengths of 64, 128, 256, 512, 1024, 2048, and 4096 bytes. In actuality, the program adds 21 bytes to each frame length to correspond to the overhead bytes which are are wrapped around the information field. Thus, the average frame length actually represents the length of the information field. The WAN operating rates, which vary from 4800 bps to 1.536 Mbps, represent commonly available analog leased line operating rates (through 19 200 bps) and commonly available digital leased line operating rates. Figure 7.4 illustrates the table generated from the execution of that program.

In examining the entries in Figure 7.4 note that the T1 operating rate of 1.536 Mbps represents the T1 speed of 1.544 Mbps less 8000 bps used for T1 framing. Also note that at

```
REM PROGRAM TRWAN.BAS
REM THIS PROGRAM COMPUTES THE MAXIMUM FRAME RATE THAT A WIDE AREA
REM NETWORK TRANSMISSION FACILITY CAN CARRY BETWEEN TWO REMOTE BRIDGES
CLS
DIM MFPS(9, 7)                                   'max frames per sec
FOR I = 1 TO 9
READ RATE(I)
NEXT I
DATA 4800,9600,19200,56000,64000,128000,256000,512000,1536000
FOR I = 1 TO 7
READ FLENGTH(I)
NEXT I
DATA 64,128,256,512,1024,2048,4096
FOR I = 1 TO 9
FOR J = 1 TO 7
MFPS(I, J) = (RATE(I) / 8) / (FLENGTH(J) + 21)
NEXT J
NEXT I
PRINT "WAN RATE          --------MAXIMUM FRAME RATE PER SECOND -----------"
PRINT "  BPS                 BASED UPON AVERAGE FRAME LENGTH IN BYTES"
PRINT "                64        128       256       512      1024      2048     409
PRINT
J = 1
FOR I = 1 TO 9
PRINT USING " ######## "; RATE(I);
PRINT USING " ####.## ####.## #####.##"; MFPS(I, 1); MFPS(I, 2); MFPS(I, 3)
PRINT USING " ####.## #####.##"; MFPS(I, 4); MFPS(I, 5);
PRINT USING " ####.## #####.##"; MFPS(I, 6); MFPS(I, 7)
NEXT I
END
```

Figure 7.3 Program listing of TRWAN.BAS.

WAN RATE	--------MAXIMUM FRAME RATE PER SECOND -----------						
BPS	BASED UPON AVERAGE FRAME LENGTH IN BYTES						
	64	128	256	512	1024	2048	4096
4800	7.06	4.03	2.17	1.13	0.57	0.29	0.15
9600	14.12	8.05	4.33	2.25	1.15	0.58	0.29
19200	28.24	16.11	8.66	4.50	2.30	1.16	0.58
56000	82.35	46.98	25.27	13.13	6.70	3.38	1.70
64000	94.12	53.69	28.88	15.01	7.66	3.87	1.94
128000	188.24	107.38	57.76	30.02	15.31	7.73	3.89
256000	376.47	214.77	115.52	60.04	30.62	15.47	7.77
512000	752.94	429.53	231.05	120.08	61.24	30.93	15.55
1536000	2258.82	1288.59	693.14	360.23	183.73	92.80	46.64

Figure 7.4 Execution results of program TRWAN.BAS.

the 1.536 Mbps rate and an average frame length of 64 bytes the maximum frame rate of 2259 fps is less than the frame rate of 2293 fps for a 260-station 4-Mbps Token-Ring network constructed using 10 000 feet of cable (see Appendix B). Thus, the WAN operating rate of a high-speed T1 circuit can be expected to function as a bottleneck for the transfer of data between Token-Ring networks without considering the effect of the overhead of the transmission protocol or the use of data compression to enhance transmission efficiency.

Protocol overhead

To illustrate the effect of a protocol's overhead upon the maximum frame rate supported by different WAN operating rates, let us revise the program TRWAN.BAS. If we assume the WAN protocol overhead is 20%, we change the computation of the two-dimensional array MFPS to

$$MFPS(I,J) = (RATE(I)/8)/((FLENGTH(J) + 21) * 1.2)$$

If you want to examine the effect of a different overhead percentage, change the multiplier 1.2 to 1.15 for computing a 15% protocol overhead, to 1.1 for a 10% protocol overhead, and so on. Figure 7.5 lists the results obtained by executing the program TRWAN.BAS in which a protocol overhead of 20% was used for frame rate computations.

WAN RATE BPS	ADJUSTED FRAME RATE BASED UPON 20 PERCENT WAN PROTOCOL OVERHEAD --------MAXIMUM FRAME RATE PER SECOND ----------- BASED UPON AVERAGE FRAME LENGTH IN BYTES						
	64	128	256	512	1024	2048	4096
4800	5.88	3.36	1.81	0.94	0.48	0.24	0.12
9600	11.76	6.71	3.61	1.88	0.96	0.48	0.24
19200	23.53	13.42	7.22	3.75	1.91	0.97	0.49
56000	68.63	39.15	21.06	10.94	5.58	2.82	1.42
64000	78.43	44.74	24.07	12.51	6.38	3.22	1.62
128000	156.86	89.49	48.13	25.02	12.76	6.44	3.24
256000	313.73	178.97	96.27	50.03	25.52	12.89	6.48
512000	627.45	357.94	192.54	100.06	51.04	25.78	12.95
1536000	1882.35	1073.83	577.62	300.19	153.11	77.33	38.86

Figure 7.5 Execution results of program TRWAN.BAS with a 20% protocol overhead.

Data compression

Due to the ability of data compression to reduce redundancies contained within the information field of a Token-Ring frame, the use of this technology increases the efficiency of the wide area network transmission facility. Since 1990 several vendors, including Newport Systems and Magnalink Communications, have introduced compression performing remote bridges. Although the effect of compression depends upon the level of data redundancy which changes from frame to frame, most vendors advertise an average compression ratio of 2:1 for their products. What this means is that the logical data carried by the information field on the average is doubled within the physical information field. Thus, to consider the effect of data compression upon the frame rate transfer capability of the wide area network transmission facility you would modify the computation of MFPS(I,J) in the program TRWAN.BAS as follows:

MFPS(I,J) = (RATE(I)/8)/(FLENGTH(J) * K + 21)

where K represents the reciprocal of the average data compression ratio. To consider the effect of both data compression and protocol overhead upon the frame transfer rate of the wide area network transmission facility, you would modify the computation of MFPS(I,J) as follows:

MFPS(I,J) = (RATE(I)/8)/((FLENGTH(J) * K + 21) * P)

where K represents the reciprocal of the average data compression ratio and P represents the average protocol overhead.

To illustrate the use of the revised computation of MFPS(I,J), let us assume that the average data compression ratio is 2 and the expected protocol overhead is 15%. Then, K has a value of 1/2 or 0.5, while P has a value of 1.15. Figure 7.6 illustrates the tabulation of frame rates obtained by modifying the computation of MFPS(I,J) as previously discussed and then executing the program TRWAN.BAS again. In comparing the tabulations contained in Figures 7.4 through 7.6, you will note that the key to reducing the potential of the wide area network transmission facility from functioning as a network bottleneck is obtained by the application of data compression. In fact, at certain operational rates the WAN transmission facility may

```
WAN RATE          --------MAXIMUM FRAME RATE PER SECOND -----------
  BPS               BASED UPON AVERAGE FRAME LENGTH IN BYTES
                 64       128      256      512     1024     2048    4096

      4800       9.84     6.14     3.50     1.88     0.98     0.50    0.25
      9600      19.69    12.28     7.00     3.77     1.96     1.00    0.50
     19200      39.38    24.55    14.01     7.53     3.92     2.00    1.01
     56000     114.85    71.61    40.85    21.97    11.42     5.82    2.94
     64000     131.26    81.84    46.69    25.11    13.05     6.66    3.36
    128000     262.51   163.68    93.38    50.23    26.10    13.31    6.72
    256000     525.02   327.37   186.75   100.46    52.21    26.63   13.45
    512000    1050.04   654.73   373.50   200.91   104.41    53.26   26.90
   1536000    3150.12  1964.19  1120.51   602.73   313.24   159.77   80.69
```

Figure 7.6 Execution results of program TRWAN.BAS using a data compression ratio of 2 and a protocol overhead of 15%.

no longer be a bottleneck. For example, from Figure 7.6 you will note that a T1 circuit is capable of transporting 3150 64-byte frames per second with a data compression ratio of 2 and a protocol overhead of 15%. In comparison, we previously noted that the frame rate on a 260-station 4-Mbps Token-Ring network constructed using 10 000 feet of cable is 2293 frames per second. Thus, this WAN link connected to compression performing remote bridges would have the capability to transfer a greater number of frames per second than the 4-Mbps Token-Ring network could generate. Readers can modify the program TRWAN.BAS and use it in conjunction with the entries in Appendix B to determine the most appropriate WAN operating rate based upon the topology, size, and operating rates of networks to be connected, as well as on the transmission protocol overhead and the expected gain in transmission efficiency due to the use of compression performing bridges or routers if this feature is included in the remote bridges or routers you are using or anticipate acquiring.

Internet traffic flow

Now that mathematical models have been developed to estimate the frame flow on individual Token-Ring networks and through the use of remote bridges and routers connected using different types of WAN transmission facilities, let's focus our attention upon the traffic flow between remotely located interconnected networks. In doing so we will use the model presented in Chapter 6 in which the total traffic flow, R_T, between networks has the following relationship to the frame rates on networks 1 (R_1) and 2 (R_2) and the wide area transmission facility frame transfer rate which we will denote as R_3:

$$\frac{1}{R_T} = \frac{1}{R_1} + \frac{1}{R_2} + \frac{1}{R_3}$$

or

$$R_T = \frac{R_1\ R_2\ R_3}{R_2\ R_3 + R_1\ R_3 + R_1\ R_2}$$

To illustrate the use of this equation, let's assume you wish to download a 640 Kbyte file from a server located on a 16-Mbps Token-Ring network which has 200 stations and 10 000 feet of cable to a 4-Mbps Token-Ring which has 50 stations and 4000 feet of cable, while the remote bridges or routers connecting each network use a 64-Kbps transmission facility. Since a file transfer uses the largest size frame available for most of the transfer, the transfer would take place using 4500-byte frames which is the largest information field length supported by both 4- and 16-Mbps Token-Ring networks. From Appendix B the closest entries we can locate govern the frame rate for a frame length of 4096 bytes. From that appendix, the maximum frame rate supported by a 4-Mbps network with 50 stations and 4000 feet of cable is 121 fps, while the maximum frame rate on a 16-Mbps network with 200 stations and 10 000 feet of cable is 471 fps. From Figure 7.5 we note that the maximum frame rate supported by a 56-Kbps digital circuit with a 20% protocol overhead is 1.42 fps when the average frame length is 4096 bytes. Using our formula to find the transfer rate, we obtain

$$R_T = \frac{121 \times 471 \times 1.42}{471 \times 1.42 + 121 \times 1.42 + 121 \times 471} = 1.399 \text{ fps}$$

As we noted in Chapter 6, this computed value of R_T represents a best-case scenario in that it assumes the transfer of data from one network to another occurs without other stations on each network using the network or requesting internet transmission. Suppose the use of a monitoring program on each network indicated that at any time an average of three workstations were using the transmission facilities of each network and two workstations were using internet transmission. Then, you would adjust the values of R_1 and R_2 by dividing each by 3, and adjust the value of R_3 by dividing its value by 2. Doing so we obtain

$$R_T = \frac{(121/3)(471/3)(1.42/2)}{(471/3) \times (1.42/2) + (121/3) \times (1.42/2) + (121/3) \times (471/3)}$$
$$= 0.69 \text{ fps}$$

Based upon the preceding you can expect a best-case frame flow between networks of 1.399 frames per second and an average frame flow between networks of 0.69 frames per second.

For an information field of 4096 bytes the maximum flow of information between networks is 4096 bytes/frame × 1.399 frames per second, or 5730 bytes per second. Then, the optimum transfer time of a 640 Kbyte file would become

$$\frac{640 \text{ Kbyte} \times 1024 \text{ bytes/K}}{4096 \text{ bytes/frame} \times 1.399 \text{ frames/second}} = 114 \text{ seconds}$$

To compute the average file transfer time we would use the average transfer rate of 0.69 frames per second. Using an information field of 4096 bytes and a frame rate of 0.69 fps, the average information transfer capability between networks becomes 4096 bytes/frame × 0.69 frames per second, i.e. 2826 bytes/second. Then, the average transfer time to move a 640 Kbyte file between networks becomes

$$\frac{640 \text{ Kbyte} \times 1024 \text{ bytes/K}}{2826 \text{ bytes/second}} = 232 \text{ seconds}$$

This indicates that the transmission time to move a 640 Kbyte file between two Token-Ring networks connected by a pair of remote bridges or routers using a 56-Kbps wide area network transmission facility can be expected on the average to be 232 seconds or slightly under four minutes. In a best-case scenario the transfer time will be 114 seconds or slightly under two minutes. Both timings are based upon the network characteristics previously discussed and will obviously change if either network or the wide area network transmission rate changes.

You can extend the previous computations to determine a peak transmission time by monitoring each network to determine the peak number of users performing network activity at a given period of time. Once you have obtained this information, you would then adjust the values for R_1, R_2, and

R_3 in a similar way to the manner in which those values were adjusted to determine the average frame transfer rate between networks. By considering the peak traffic on each network, your computation for R_T would result in a worst-case frame transfer rate which you could use to compute the maximum file transfer time.

Whether or not the optimum, average, and peak transfer times are acceptable depends upon your organization and its need for speed. While an increase in the WAN operating rate will have a significant effect upon the ability to transfer frames between networks, it is not without cost. Thus, you may wish to perform a cost analysis to determine if a reduction in file transfer time or an increase in the transfer capability of the WAN is worth the expense associated with obtaining a higher wide area network transmission capability. In addition, you should consider the relationship of file transfer activity in the form of programs and data files to the transfer of relatively short electronic messages in the form of files. For example, if the primary use of the internet is to transport short electronic mail files, would an additional expense of $1000 or more per month to reduce the transfer time of a message from three seconds to one second be worthwhile? Considering the fact that it may take a second or two for a person to move his or her hand to the keyboard and press a key to 'open the mail', I would probably defer the expense. However, the answers to such questions are for you to decide. In doing so you can use the models provided in this book to determine transfer rates and transfer times and use that information in conjunction with the cost of communications equipment and transmission facilities as your decision criteria.

8

TRANSMISSION OPTIMIZATION TECHNIQUES

Until now, the primary focus of this book was upon the creation and use of mathematical models to predict the performance of different types of local area networks and internetworking devices. In this chapter we will turn our attention to the use of several optimization techniques which, when incorporated into bridges and routers, will enhance the efficiency of internet transmission. In addition, we will examine the use of different types of network interface cards or adapters, which when used in a workstation enhance its ability to transfer information onto and receive information from the network.

Techniques we will examine in this chapter include the use of filtering, precedence and express queuing, data compression, frame truncation, and the switched telephone network to supplement the use of leased lines during peak transmission periods. Readers should note that most remote bridge and router manufacturers provide one or more of the techniques described in this chapter. However, readers should also note that the efficiency of the implementation of each technique varies between vendors. In addition, most vendors provide only a small subset of the techniques covered in this chapter. Since the value of each technique is based upon your specific networking requirements, you will have to compare the operational results of each technique against your specific communications environment to determine which techniques provide a higher level of networking capability, and you can then use this chapter as a guide in your equipment selection process.

In examining network interface cards our focus of attention will be upon different hardware design features and the effect of those features upon the data transfer capability of the adapter. You can also use this information as a guide to facilitate your equipment selection process.

8.1 FILTERING

Filtering is the most common transmission optimization technique incorporated into remote bridges and routers. Although most devices support a predefined filtering capability in which source and/or destination frame addresses are entered into a filtering table during the equipment installation process, other devices permit an authorized administrator to dynamically change the filtering tables since few networks are static.

Local vs remote filtering

Through the use of filtering you can control the number and types of packets that are forwarded across a transmission circuit linking two remote bridges or routers. Although you can also use filtering to control the flow of data between two local area networks connected by a local bridge, we will focus our attention upon the application of filtering by devices interconnected via wide area transmission facilities. This is because the application of filtering by devices connected via wide area transmission facilities directly affects the required transmission rate linking the filtering devices. Since the monthly cost of a wide area transmission facility is proportional to its operating rate, the ability to lower the required operating rate through the use of filtering can be expected to reduce your organization's transmission cost. In comparison, the use of filtering by a local bridge has a less significant effect. First, it usually has no effect upon cost since local cabling links each network at the common local bridge as illustrated at the top of Figure 8.1. Secondly, the use of filtering has a lesser effect upon performance when performed by a local bridge than when performed by a remote bridge. This is because the WAN link connecting two remote bridges or routers operates at a fraction of the operating rate of each network. Thus, the removal of

Local bridging

Filtering has no effect upon the cabling used to connect local networks. Since both networks operate at Mbps rates the removal of frames based on filtering usually has a negligible effect upon network performance.

Remote bridging

Filtering can have a significant effect upon the operating rate of a circuit connecting geographically dispersed networks since the WAN link normally operates at a fraction of each LAN operating rate.

Figure 8.1 Effect of local vs remote bridge filtering.

frames via filtering as illustrated in the lower portion of Figure 8.1 has a more pronounced effect upon a lower operating rate circuit than local cable connecting two higher operating rate local area networks.

Filtering methods

There are several types of filtering supported by bridges and routers. Two of the most common methods of filtering frames are based upon the use of address and service fields in a frame.

Address field filtering

The most basic type of filtering is performed by bridges which operate at the MAC sublayer of the OSI Reference Model's data link layer. Operating at this layer bridges are transparent to high-level protocols which function at the network layer of the OSI Reference Model. Thus, the primary mechanism used for filtering is based upon the use of the destination and source address fields within Token-Ring and Ethernet/IEEE 802.3 frames. For example, consider the IEEE Token-Ring functional addresses listed in Table 2.4 in Chapter 2. Assume you wanted to preclude the transmission of Token-Ring functional address frames from being forwarded onto the Ethernet network illustrated in Figure 8.1 since those frames normally are irrelevant to stations on the Ethernet network. To do so you would set your bridge to filter all frames with destination addresses equivalent to the block of destination addresses assigned by the IEEE to the Token-Ring functional addresses listed in Table 2.4.

To illustrate the effect of functional address filtering, consider the active monitor address listed in Table 2.4. The active monitor on a Token-Ring network transmits an active monitor frame every seven seconds, or 12 343 times each day. This frame is used to notify the standby monitors that the active monitor is operational and the frame is irrelevant to an Ethernet network. Thus, the filtering of just this one frame reduces the flow of data from a Token-Ring network onto an Ethernet network by approximately 13 000 frames per day. Even when two Token-Ring networks are interconnected active monitor frames should be filtered as each network has its own active monitor. Thus, this filtering example is applicable to both Token-Ring to Ethernet as well as Token-Ring to Token-Ring bridging.

Service access point filtering

Filtering based upon destination and source address fields is supported by essentially all bridges. A more sophisticated level of filtering supported by some bridges is based upon the DSAP and SSAP addresses carried within the information field of Token-Ring and Ethernet/IEEE 802.3 frames.

Figure 8.2 illustrates the general format of the conversion of a Token-Ring frame into an Ethernet frame. The DSAP and SSAP can be considered post office boxes which identify locations where information is left and received to and from higher level layers of the OSI Reference Model. For example, the transportation of an electronic mail message used by a higher network process would have a defined DSAP. Thus, a

Figure 8.2 Token-Ring to IEEE 802.3 frame conversion. The conversion of a Token-Ring frame to an IEEE 802.3 frame results in the copying of the contents of the destination and source address fields as well as the subfields within the information field.

bridge which includes the capability to perform filtering based upon DSAP and SSAP addresses would provide you with the ability to perform filtering at the application level as well as to add a degree of security to your internet if you wish to restrict the movement of frames carrying certain types of information between networks.

8.2 PRECEDENCE AND EXPRESS QUEUING

In Chapter 4 we examined the use of waiting line analysis or queuing to determine an optimum line operating rate to link remote bridges and routers, the effect of single- and dual-port equipment upon internet performance, and buffer memory requirements of network devices. In doing so we assumed that the servicing of queues was based upon a first-in, first-out basis. That is, the arrival of frame n followed by frame $n + 1$ into a queue would result in a remote bridge or router transmitting frame n prior to transmitting frame $n + 1$. Although most remote bridges and routers operate on a first-in, first-out service basis, other devices may support precedence and/or express queuing. In doing so they provide a level of performance which may considerably exceed the performance of other devices that do not support such queuing options during periods of peak network activity. To illustrate the advantages of precedence and express queuing, let us first focus our attention upon the operation of first-in, first-out queuing and some of the problems associated with this queuing method.

First-in, first-out queuing

When first-in, first-out queuing is used messages are queued in the order in which they are received. This is the simplest method of queuing as a single physical and logical buffer area is used to store data and all messages are assumed to have the same priority of service. The software used by the bridge or router simply extracts each frame based upon its position in the queue. Figure 8.3 illustrates first-in, first-out queuing.

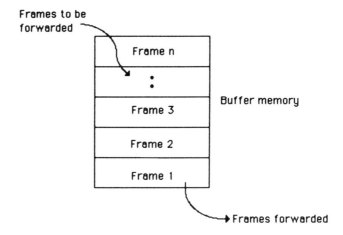

Figure 8.3 First-in, first-out queuing, in which frames are forwarded in their order of arrival into buffer memory.

Queuing problems

The major problems associated with first-in, first-out queuing involve the effect of this queuing method upon a mixture of interactive and batch internet transmission during peak network utilization periods. To illustrate the problems associated with first-in, first-out queuing consider the internet illustrated in Figure 8.4 in which a Token-Ring network is connected to an Ethernet network through the use of a pair of remote bridges.

Mixing file transfer and interactive sessions

Let us assume that station E on the Ethernet initiates a file transfer to station C on the Token-Ring. Let us also assume that

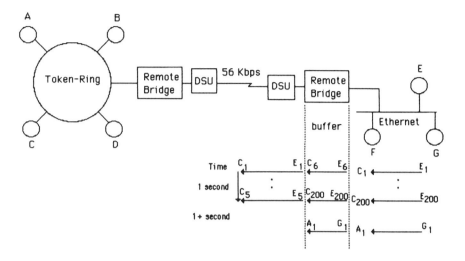

Figure 8.4 First-in, first-out queuing delays. First-in, first-out queuing can seriously degrade transmission when an interactive query occurs after the initiation of a long file transfer operation.

the Ethernet network is a 10BASE-T network operating at 10 Mbps and the wide area network transmission facility operates at 56 Kbps.

If the stations on the Ethernet are IBM PC or compatible computers with industry standard architecture (ISA) Ethernet adapter boards, the maximum transfer rate is normally less than 300 000 bytes per second. Using that figure and assuming station E transmitted for one second in which each frame was the maximum length of 1500 information field bytes, not including frame overhead, a total of 300 000 bytes/1500 bytes per frame, or 200 frames, would be presented to the remote bridge. At 56 Kbps the bridge would forward 56 000/(8 × 1500), or approximately five frames, not considering the WAN protocol and frame overhead. Thus, at the end of one second there could be 195 frames in the bridge's buffer as illustrated in the lower right portion of Figure 8.4.

Now let us assume that slightly after this one second has passed station G on the Ethernet transmits a query to an application operating on station A on the Token-Ring. The 195 frames in the buffer of the remote bridge would require approximately 40 seconds (195 frames × 1500 bytes/frame × 8 bits/byte÷56 000 bps) to be emptied from the buffer and placed onto the line prior to the frame from station G being placed onto the line. Thus, first-in, first-out queuing can seriously degrade transmission from an Ethernet to another Ethernet or to a Token-Ring network when file transfer and interactive transmission occurs between networks. The reverse situation in which transmission is from a Token-Ring to an Ethernet or between two Token-Ring networks does not result in such significant problems, since a priority mechanism is built into the Token-Ring frame which results in a more equitable shared use of the network bandwidth than is achievable on an Ethernet network.

Workstation retransmissions

In the preceding example we noted the potential for the delay of 40 seconds until data from station G was transmitted. In actuality this will almost never happen, since most remote bridges and routers have installation guidelines which typically suggest that you configure buffer memory to store only a few seconds' worth of data. However, doing so results in a workstation attempting to transfer a file retransmitting frames that were not accepted by the bridge or router, adding to network traffic as well as on the level of network utilization. This will have a detrimental effect upon a series of stations attempting concurrent file transfer operations as well as stations performing interactive client–server activities when file transfer operations are in effect. In certain situations buffer queuing delays added to frame retransmission time can result in file transfer timeouts which result in the termination of the file transfer session. In other situations, random delays in interactive sessions will frustrate network users. Due to such problems some remote bridge and router manufacturers have incorporated precedence queuing and express queuing into their products.

Precedence queuing

Precedence queuing was probably the first method used by remote bridge and router manufacturers to enhance the transmission of internet traffic through device buffer memory. Under precedence queuing data entering a communications device, such as a remote bridge or router, is sorted by priority into separate queues as illustrated in Figure 8.5. Since a bridge operates at the MAC sublayer of the OSI Reference Model's

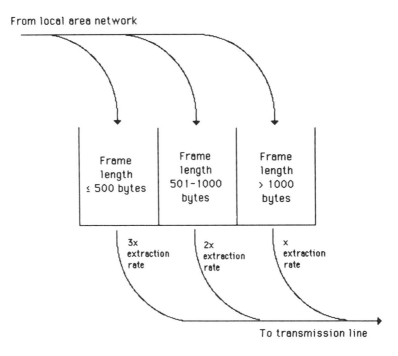

Figure 8.5 Precedence queuing based upon frame length. Frames are placed into logical queues based upon their length. In this example, the Ethernet information field length was used as the queue placement variable. Service of the queues can be on a round-robin or a priority basis, with the latter shown in this example.

data link layer, a logical question many readers probably have concerns the method by which a bridge can recognize different frame priorities.

Methods used

In actuality, a remote bridge performing precedence queuing does not look for a priority byte as there is none to look for. Instead, the bridge can use one of two methods—examining the DSAP address in a frame or the frame length. The examination of DSAP addresses permits the bridge to recognize certain predefined applications and prioritize the routing of frames onto the wide area network transmission facility based upon those priorities. The second method which is based upon the frame length presumes that interactive traffic is carried by shorter length frames than file transfer and program load traffic.

Operation

Figure 8.5 illustrates the operation of precedence queuing based upon frame length within the buffer area of a remote bridge. In this example the physical buffer area is subdivided into logical partitions, with each partition used to queue frames whose length falls within a predefined range of values.

Frames from the attached local area network are placed into logical partitions based upon the length of the frame. For an Ethernet network this could entail subdivision of the maximum length of 1500 bytes of the information field of that frame. Once logical queues are formed the servicing of the queues can occur on a round-robin or a priority basis. The lower portion of Figure 8.5 illustrates a priority extraction process in which for every frame whose length exceeds 1000 bytes which is serviced and placed on the transmission line two frames with a length of 501 to 1000 bytes and three frames whose length is less than or equal to 500 bytes are serviced from their queues and placed on the transmission line.

Express queuing

Express queuing is a term used by one bridge and router manufacturer to represent the allocation of transmission bandwidth based upon the destination address of frames in the queue as well as the number of frames with the same destination address in the queue. That is, under express queuing transmission bandwidth is allocated so that in any given interval of time each destination address will be assigned to either a fixed portion of the WAN bandwidth or a smaller portion if there are fewer frames queued with that destination address. This technique recognizes the fact that interactive transmission is represented by a low rate of frame flow. Therefore, this type of transmission only requires a portion of the total transmission bandwidth to obtain an acceptable flow over the wide area transmission facility. The actual method by which bandwidth is allocated is based upon an algorithm designed not only to provide interactive transmission priority service but also to ensure that multiple concurrent file transfers share the majority of the remaining bandwidth in an equitable manner which prevents timeouts from occurring.

8.3 DATA COMPRESSION

Unless data is purely random it contains a degree of redundancy. Data compression can be considered a process which uses one or more algorithms to reduce or eliminate data redundancies.

Compression ratio

The efficiency of compression is referred to as the compression ratio, which represents the ratio of the number of original bytes in a frame to the number of compressed bytes. A high compression ratio represents either efficient compression, data with a high level of redundancy, or both.

Since data carried by information frames varies over time with respect to their content and amount of data redundancy, the compression ratio will also vary over time. Normally you can expect a compression-performing remote bridge or router to have an average compression ratio between 2.0 and 2.5. Allowing for the fact that the wide area network transmission protocol has a 10–20% overhead, the effect of compression typically results in the doubling of the information-carrying capacity of a circuit. That is, as a general rule you can expect a 56-Kbps digital circuit to transfer an average of 112 Kbps of LAN frame data when compression-performing remote bridges or routers are used.

Compression methods

There are three main categories into which compression methods fall—byte-oriented, statistical, and table lookup or dictionary-based.

Byte-oriented

Byte-oriented compression techniques examine the bit composition of each byte, comparing the composition of the current byte to one or more succeeding bytes. If redundancies are noted, the algorithm replaces a series of bytes with a new sequence which eliminates those redundancies. A few of the more popular byte-oriented compression techniques include run length encoding, half-byte encoding, and null suppression.

Null suppression simply results in the substitution of a compression-indicating character and null count character for a sequence of nulls. In comparison, run length encoding permits any character sequence to be reduced by the use of a three-character sequence to replace a repeated run of any character. The three-character sequence includes a compression-indicating character, the character in the run, and a count character.

Half-byte encoding is a compression technique which results in the replacement of a sequence of characters that has the same half-byte bit composition, such as a string of numerics, by encoding two numerics into a byte. Then, the reduced byte sequence is prefixed by a compression-indicating character and a count byte. Readers are referred to the author's book *Data Compression (third edition)*, published by John Wiley & Sons, for detailed information concerning the operation of byte-oriented, statistical, and dictionary-based compression algorithms as well as for examples of program code used to implement different compression techniques.

Statistical

Statistical compression algorithms replace frequently occurring bytes by short codes and less frequently occurring bytes by longer codes. The net result of this replacement process is to reduce the average number of bits required to represent a character from eight to a lesser number, typically between four and five, resulting in a compression ratio of 2:1 or less. In replacing each fixed length byte of eight bits, the replacement process results in the use of a variable length code. This variable length code is constructed based upon a statistical compression algorithm, the Huffman coding technique being the most popular method employed. This technique results in the encoded compressed data bits having a prefix property which makes it instantaneously decodable. Thus, decompression performed according to the Huffman algorithm minimizes delays in comparison to the use of other compression methods. While this was an important consideration during the era of Intel 8088 microprocessors, the widespread availability of Intel 80486 and other modern high-performance microprocessors has reduced the decompression times associated with other compression techniques to the point where they do not adversely affect the throughput of data. Readers are again referred to the author's book *Data Compression (third edition)*, published by John Wiley & Sons, for information concerning Huffman coding of data and the instantaneous decoding of such data.

Dictionary-based

Since the replacement of frequently occurring bytes by short codes and less frequently occurring bytes by longer codes results in a reduction in the average number of bits required to represent a character, it is logical to assume greater efficiencies can be obtained by substituting codes for strings of characters. This logic resulted in the development of dictionary-based compression algorithms in which transmitted data is placed into a dictionary and the location of characters and strings of characters (pointers) is transmitted instead of the actual data.

The most popular dictionary-based compression algorithm originates from the work of Jacob Ziv and Abraham Lempel at Hafia University during the late 1970s. More modern versions of their algorithm are referred to as Lempel–Ziv or LZ-based and differ in the method used to flush the dictionary, the number of pointers and size of the dictionary, and how pointers are coded in the compressed output.

One popular version of LZ coding is more commonly known as Lempel–Ziv–Welsh and is the method used in the CCITT V.42bis modem compression standard.

Performance considerations

Although compression is standardized for use in modems, the same is not true for its use in remote bridges and routers. This means not only that vendor compression performing equipment will more likely than not fail to interoperate but, in addition, you may have to rely upon vendor performance data. Unfortunately, some vendors have a tendency to place their equipment performance in the best possible light by transmitting files with a considerable degree of data redundancy and then claiming a high compression ratio, such as 4:1 or 5:1. If compression is an important equipment acquisition consideration, the author suggests that you create a set of files that are representative of your internet traffic and have each vendor under consideration transfer those files and provide you with either their transmission time at a fixed WAN rate or their compression ratio.

8.4 ETHERNET FRAME TRUNCATION

As noted in Chapter 2, Ethernet frames require a minimum length of 64 bytes even when the frame carries just one information character. Thus, a query/response client–server communications session in which a workstation user on an Ethernet initiates queries by entering a few search characters results in the transmission of a frame with a large number of pad characters to ensure the minimum packet size of 64 bytes is reached.

Overhead

While the overhead associated with the use of pad characters is relatively insignificant on a 10-Mbps 10BASE-T network, those pad characters become more significant when frames are directed across a wide area transmission facility operating at a fraction of the local area network operating rate. Recognizing the effect of padded Ethernet frames upon communications over WAN facilities, Advanced Computer Communications was among the first vendors to offer Ethernet frame truncation in their remote bridge and router products.

The use of frame truncation results in Ethernet padded frames having their pad characters removed prior to transmission over a WAN. This results in the transmission of reduced length frames which require less time to transmit. This technique also permits the remote bridge or router to strip pad characters from minimum length Ethernet frames as they are placed in memory, permitting more frames to be stored in memory as well as the faster servicing of frames when they are packeted and placed on the transmission line.

Utilization example

As an example of the potential benefit obtained from the use of Ethernet frame truncation, consider a situation in which 20 stations on an Ethernet have users interactively working with a program located on a remote Token-Ring network through remote bridges communicating at 19 200 bps. Let us assume a worst-case scenario in which each user simultaneously enters a query using a five-digit invoice number. Then, instead of five characters in the information field, each frame must contain 46 characters, including pad characters to comply with the Ethernet minimum packet length standard. Without considering the overhead of the protocol used for transmitting frames from the Ethernet to the Token-Ring network, this worst-case situation results in 20 × 46, or 920 bytes, being presented to the remote bridge or router when only 20 × 5, or 100 bytes, actually require transmission. Then, the interactive traffic would use 920 × 8/19 200, or approximately 38%, of the WAN bandwidth without Ethernet frame truncation. With Ethernet frame truncation, transmission would be reduced to 100 bytes which would use 100 × 8/19 200, or approximately 4%, of the WAN bandwidth.

8.5 SWITCHED NETWORK USE FOR OVERCOMING CONGESTION

One problem frequently encountered by network designers, managers, and analysts is determining the operating rate of a wide area network transmission facility. Almost all WAN transmission facilities are either leased analog or digital lines whose monthly cost is proportional to the data transmission rate they provide. Most organizations typically attempt to determine their busy hour traffic and obtain a wide area network transmission facility which provides an acceptable level of performance during the busy hour. While this is a valid network design technique, it does not consider the use of a new class of equipment known as bandwidth-on-demand inverse multiplexers (BODM) nor the fact that in many organizations busy hour transmission may considerably exceed normal transmission.

Using bandwidth-on-demand inverse multiplexers

To illustrate the use of bandwidth-on-demand inverse multi-plexers, as well as a feature known as dial-on congestion incorporated into some remote bridges and routers, let us assume our network analysts determined that a fractional T1 line operating at 128 Kbps was required to interconnect two remote bridges at a cost of $4500 per month. Let us also assume that the cost of switched 56 Kbps transmission is $30 per hour and that during an eight-hour day the WAN facility requires only 128 Kbps of bandwidth for 90 minutes, while for the remainder of the workday a bandwidth of 64 Kbps or less provides an acceptable level of performance.

Figure 8.6 illustrates the use of bandwidth-on-demand inverse multiplexers which examine the flow of packets between remote bridges. As the flow of packets increases to the point where there is essentially no available bandwidth on the leased line for a predefined period of time the multiplexer initiates a switched 56-Kbps call to the distant multiplexer. Based upon our assumed cost of $30 per hour, switched 56-Kbps transmission for 90 minutes per day would result in a daily cost of $45, or $990 if there are 22 working days in the month. If a 64-Kbps fractional T1 line costs $2800 per month, the total cost of using a 64-Kbps leased line and supplementing its capacity via the use of switched 56-Kbps service would be $3790, not including the cost of the bandwidth-on-demand inverse multiplexers. Thus, in this example the use of BODM equipment would result in a monthly line cost reduction of $710.

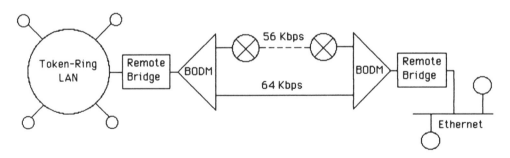

Figure 8.6 Using bandwidth-on-demand inverse multiplexers. A bandwidth-on-demand inverse multiplexer can be configured to support a leased line and initiate one or more switched 56-Kbps calls when the activity on the leased line exceeds a predefined threshold for a defined period of time.

Dial-on congestion

To alleviate the cost of separate bandwidth-on-demand inverse multiplexers several vendors manufacturing remote bridges and routers have incorporated a dial-on-congestion capability into their products. This feature results in the use of a second port on a remote bridge or router for switched dial use during peak periods of activity. Users are referred to the author's book *Data Communications Networking Devices (third edition)*, published by John Wiley & Sons, for additional information concerning the use of inverse multiplexers.

8.6 NETWORK INTERFACE CARD

The network interface card is a circuit board designed for insertion into the expansion slot of a specific type of computer, such as an IBM PC or compatible computer, a Micro Channel IBM PS/2 computer, or an Apple Macintosh. This card contains a series of chips or an integrated chip set which implements the network access protocol, as well as RAM memory, and other chips designed to perform specific functions which can have a considerable bearing upon the ability of the adapter card to transfer data onto and receive data from the network.

Performance considerations

The key to the ability of a network interface card to transfer data onto and from a network is the method by which data transfer occurs between the adapter card and the computer in which it is inserted. Data transfer between the adapter card and the computer can be implemented in several ways, including direct memory access (DMA), I/O mapped, and shared memory.

DMA interface

A direct memory access (DMA) interface is a data transfer technique in which the transfer of data between the adapter card and the computer's memory can occur simultaneously with other operations. To accomplish this the DMA transfer is initiated by a board processor storing a starting and ending address and then initiating a DMA transfer operation, after which the processor can perform other operations during which data is transferred from the adapter card's memory to the workstation's memory. If the adapter card does not include an onboard processor, circuitry can be used to implement a DMA transfer. To accomplish this, an on-board buffer area on the adapter card receives data from the network. As the buffer fills, circuitry on the adapter recognizes this condition as a signal to generate a DMA transfer.

Although a DMA transfer permits the simultaneous transfer of data from the NIC to the computer's memory to occur with other operations, it is generally slow in comparison to other methods of data transfer. The reason for this is due to the time required to set up and initiate a DMA transfer. A second factor which limits the capability of a DMA transfer is the fact that it requires contiguous memory in the host computer for its transfer operations. Since frames are often assembled from several different areas in memory, each DMA transfer may be limited to the amount of data that can be transferred.

I/O mapping

I/O mapping is a data transfer mechanism based upon the shared use of an I/O port between the adapter card and the host computer. This method of data transfer is faster than the use of a DMA transfer as it occurs at the I/O channel speed and eliminates the DMA transfer setup time.

Shared memory

In a shared memory method of data transfer a portion of the computer's memory is set up so that it can be used by both the adapter card and the computer. This results in a frame avoiding an actual transfer between the adapter and the computer, enhancing the data transfer between the computer and the network.

Most modern high performance network adapter cards use some type of shared memory scheme to expedite the transfer of data from the computer to the network and vice versa.

Typically, shared memory can be set up in increments of 16 Kbytes, from 16 to 64 Kbytes. Since the use of a LAN program and an application program will typically use a majority of conventional memory, many computers are limited to a setup in which only 16 Kbytes are used as shared memory. While this amount of memory will not adversely affect the operation of NICs connected to a 4-Mbps Token-Ring or a 10-Mbps Ethernet network, the opposite can occur if you are connected to a 16-Mbps Token-Ring network. This is because the 16-Mbps Token-

Ring network can have an information frame whose length can exceed 16 Kbytes.

In comparing the method used by the NIC for transferring data, performance can significantly differ depending upon the technique used. Although you may be tempted to simply select a vendor's adapter card based upon their stated data transfer rate, there is one additional item you should consider prior to doing so. That additional item is the transfer rate of the hard disk of the computer in which you intend to install the network interface card.

The transfer rate of the hard disk will vary with the type of disk and disk controller used as well as with the bus interface of your computer. For example, older PC XT computers have a disk I/O transfer capability under 1 Mbps. Thus, installing a shared memory network interface card with a 2-Mbps transfer capability would probably be extravagant, since any sustained transfer of data to or from the computer's hard disk would be limited to 1 Mbps regardless of the type of NIC used. Thus, you should select a network interface card in conjunction with the performance characteristics of the computer in which it is to be installed.

APPENDIX A

P(N) AND P(N>K) VALUES FOR SINGLE-CHANNEL, SINGLE-SERVER SYSTEM

The program SSERVER.BAS whose statements are listed in Figure A.1 was developed to provide a listing of the probability of N units and the probability of K or more units in a single-channel, single-server system based upon different server utilization levels. The results obtained from the execution of SSERVER.BAS are contained in the remaining portion of this appendix and can be used by readers to determine the buffer storage requirements of remote bridges and routers. Readers are referred to Chapter 4 for specific information concerning the use of the tables of $P(N)$ and $P(N > K)$ presented in this appendix.

```
REM PROGRAM SSERVER.BAS
CLS
PRINT "SINGLE CHANNEL SINGLE SERVER QUEUING COMPUTATION PROGRAM"
INPUT "Enter number of transactions              : ", T
INPUT "Enter time period of transactions in hours: ", H
INPUT "Enter operating rate of server in bps      : ", BPS
INPUT "Enter average frame size in bytes          : ", BYTES
ARRIVAL = T / (H * 60 * 60)
MST = BYTES * 8 / BPS
SERVICERATE = 1 / MST
UTILIZATION = ARRIVAL / SERVICERATE
PO = 1 - UTILIZATION
L = ARRIVAL / (SERVICERATE - ARRIVAL)
LQ = UTILIZATION ^ 2 / (1 - UTILIZATION)
W = 1 / (SERVICERATE - ARRIVAL)
WQ = ARRIVAL / (SERVICERATE * (SERVICERATE - ARRIVAL))
PRINT
PRINT USING "ARRIVAL RATE = ###.#### FRAMES PER SEC "; ARRIVAL
PRINT USING "SERVICE RATE = ###.#### FRAMES PER SEC "; SERVICERATE
PRINT USING "UTILIZATION  = ###.#### PERCENT"; UTILIZATION * 100
PRINT
PRINT USING "MEAN NUMBER OF FRAMES IN SYSTEM = ###.#### "; L
PRINT USING "MEAN NUMBER OF FRAMES IN QUEUE  = ###.#### "; LQ
PRINT
PRINT USING "MEAN TIME IN THE SYSTEM IN SEC = ###.#### "; W
PRINT USING "MEAN TIME IN THE QUEUE IN SEC  = ###.#### "; WQ
PRINT
END
```

Figure A.1

Probability of N units and K or more units in system based upon server utilization level ranging from 10 to 95%

For a utilization level of 10%			
Probability of N units		Probability of K or more units	
N	P(N)	K	P(N>K)
0	0.89999998	0	1.00000000
1	0.09000000	1	0.10000000
2	0.00900000	2	0.01000000
3	0.00090000	3	0.00100000
4	0.00009000	4	0.00010000
5	0.00000900	5	0.00001000
6	0.00000090	6	0.00000100
7	0.00000009	7	0.00000010
8	0.00000001	8	0.00000001
9	0.00000000	9	0.00000000
10	0.00000000	10	0.00000000
11	0.00000000	11	0.00000000
12	0.00000000	12	0.00000000
13	0.00000000	13	0.00000000
14	0.00000000	14	0.00000000
15	0.00000000	15	0.00000000
16	0.00000000	16	0.00000000
17	0.00000000	17	0.00000000
18	0.00000000	18	0.00000000
19	0.00000000	19	0.00000000
20	0.00000000	20	0.00000000
21	0.00000000	21	0.00000000
22	0.00000000	22	0.00000000
23	0.00000000	23	0.00000000
24	0.00000000	24	0.00000000
25	0.00000000	25	0.00000000

For a utilization level of 15%			
Probability of N units		Probability of K or more units	
N	P(N)	K	P(N>K)
0	0.85000002	0	1.00000000
1	0.12750000	1	0.15000001
2	0.01912500	2	0.02250000
3	0.00286875	3	0.00337500
4	0.00043031	4	0.00050625
5	0.00006455	5	0.00007594
6	0.00000968	6	0.00001139
7	0.00000145	7	0.00000171
8	0.00000022	8	0.00000026
9	0.00000003	9	0.00000004
10	0.00000000	10	0.00000001
11	0.00000000	11	0.00000000
12	0.00000000	12	0.00000000
13	0.00000000	13	0.00000000
14	0.00000000	14	0.00000000
15	0.00000000	15	0.00000000
16	0.00000000	16	0.00000000
17	0.00000000	17	0.00000000
18	0.00000000	18	0.00000000
19	0.00000000	19	0.00000000
20	0.00000000	20	0.00000000
21	0.00000000	21	0.00000000
22	0.00000000	22	0.00000000
23	0.00000000	23	0.00000000
24	0.00000000	24	0.00000000
25	0.00000000	25	0.00000000

For a utilization level of 20%

Probability of N units		Probability of K or more units	
N	P(N)	K	P(N>K)
0	0.80000001	0	1.00000000
1	0.16000000	1	0.20000000
2	0.03200000	2	0.04000000
3	0.00640000	3	0.00800000
4	0.00128000	4	0.00160000
5	0.00025600	5	0.00032000
6	0.00005120	6	0.00006400
7	0.00001024	7	0.00001280
8	0.00000205	8	0.00000256
9	0.00000041	9	0.00000051
10	0.00000008	10	0.00000010
11	0.00000002	11	0.00000002
12	0.00000000	12	0.00000000
13	0.00000000	13	0.00000000
14	0.00000000	14	0.00000000
15	0.00000000	15	0.00000000
16	0.00000000	16	0.00000000
17	0.00000000	17	0.00000000
18	0.00000000	18	0.00000000
19	0.00000000	19	0.00000000
20	0.00000000	20	0.00000000
21	0.00000000	21	0.00000000
22	0.00000000	22	0.00000000
23	0.00000000	23	0.00000000
24	0.00000000	24	0.00000000
25	0.00000000	25	0.00000000

For a utilization level of 25%

Probability of N units		Probability of K or more units	
N	P(N)	K	P(N>K)
0	0.75000000	0	1.00000000
1	0.18750000	1	0.25000000
2	0.04687500	2	0.06250000
3	0.01171875	3	0.01562500
4	0.00292969	4	0.00390625
5	0.00073242	5	0.00097656
6	0.00018311	6	0.00024414
7	0.00004578	7	0.00006104
8	0.00001144	8	0.00001526
9	0.00000286	9	0.00000381
10	0.00000072	10	0.00000095
11	0.00000018	11	0.00000024
12	0.00000004	12	0.00000006
13	0.00000001	13	0.00000001
14	0.00000000	14	0.00000000
15	0.00000000	15	0.00000000
16	0.00000000	16	0.00000000
17	0.00000000	17	0.00000000
18	0.00000000	18	0.00000000
19	0.00000000	19	0.00000000
20	0.00000000	20	0.00000000
21	0.00000000	21	0.00000000
22	0.00000000	22	0.00000000
23	0.00000000	23	0.00000000
24	0.00000000	24	0.00000000
25	0.00000000	25	0.00000000

For a utilization level of 30%

Probability of N units		Probability of K or more units	
N	P(N)	K	P(N>K)
0	0.69999999	0	1.00000000
1	0.21000001	1	0.30000001
2	0.06300000	2	0.09000000
3	0.01890000	3	0.02700000
4	0.00567000	4	0.00810000
5	0.00170100	5	0.00243000
6	0.00051030	6	0.00072900
7	0.00015309	7	0.00021870
8	0.00004593	8	0.00006561
9	0.00001378	9	0.00001968
10	0.00000413	10	0.00000590
11	0.00000124	11	0.00000177
12	0.00000037	12	0.00000053
13	0.00000011	13	0.00000016
14	0.00000003	14	0.00000005
15	0.00000001	15	0.00000001
16	0.00000000	16	0.00000000
17	0.00000000	17	0.00000000
18	0.00000000	18	0.00000000
19	0.00000000	19	0.00000000
20	0.00000000	20	0.00000000
21	0.00000000	21	0.00000000
22	0.00000000	22	0.00000000
23	0.00000000	23	0.00000000
24	0.00000000	24	0.00000000
25	0.00000000	25	0.00000000

For a utilization level of 35%

Probability of N units		Probability of K or more units	
N	P(N)	K	P(N>K)
0	0.64999998	0	1.00000000
1	0.22750001	1	0.35000002
2	0.07962501	2	0.12250002
3	0.02786876	3	0.04287501
4	0.00975406	4	0.01500625
5	0.00341392	5	0.00525219
6	0.00119487	6	0.00183827
7	0.00041821	7	0.00064339
8	0.00014637	8	0.00022519
9	0.00005123	9	0.00007882
10	0.00001793	10	0.00002759
11	0.00000628	11	0.00000965
12	0.00000220	12	0.00000338
13	0.00000077	13	0.00000118
14	0.00000027	14	0.00000041
15	0.00000009	15	0.00000014
16	0.00000003	16	0.00000005
17	0.00000001	17	0.00000002
18	0.00000000	18	0.00000001
19	0.00000000	19	0.00000000
20	0.00000000	20	0.00000000
21	0.00000000	21	0.00000000
22	0.00000000	22	0.00000000
23	0.00000000	23	0.00000000
24	0.00000000	24	0.00000000
25	0.00000000	25	0.00000000

For a utilization level of 40%

Probability of N units		Probability of K or more units	
N	P(N)	K	P(N>K)
0	0.59999996	0	1.00000000
1	0.24000001	1	0.40000004
2	0.09600001	2	0.16000003
3	0.03840001	3	0.06400002
4	0.01536000	4	0.02560001
5	0.00614400	5	0.01024000
6	0.00245760	6	0.00409600
7	0.00098304	7	0.00163840
8	0.00039322	8	0.00065536
9	0.00015729	9	0.00026214
10	0.00006291	10	0.00010486
11	0.00002517	11	0.00004194
12	0.00001007	12	0.00001678
13	0.00000403	13	0.00000671
14	0.00000161	14	0.00000268
15	0.00000064	15	0.00000107
16	0.00000026	16	0.00000043
17	0.00000010	17	0.00000017
18	0.00000004	18	0.00000007
19	0.00000002	19	0.00000003
20	0.00000001	20	0.00000001
21	0.00000000	21	0.00000000
22	0.00000000	22	0.00000000
23	0.00000000	23	0.00000000
24	0.00000000	24	0.00000000
25	0.00000000	25	0.00000000

For a utilization level of 45%

Probability of N units		Probability of K or more units	
N	P(N)	K	P(N>K)
0	0.54999995	0	1.00000000
1	0.24750000	1	0.45000005
2	0.11137501	2	0.20250005
3	0.05011876	3	0.09112503
4	0.02255345	4	0.04100627
5	0.01014905	5	0.01845282
6	0.00456707	6	0.00830377
7	0.00205518	7	0.00373670
8	0.00092483	8	0.00168151
9	0.00041617	9	0.00075668
10	0.00018728	10	0.00034051
11	0.00008428	11	0.00015323
12	0.00003792	12	0.00006895
13	0.00001707	13	0.00003103
14	0.00000768	14	0.00001396
15	0.00000346	15	0.00000628
16	0.00000156	16	0.00000283
17	0.00000070	17	0.00000127
18	0.00000031	18	0.00000057
19	0.00000014	19	0.00000026
20	0.00000006	20	0.00000012
21	0.00000003	21	0.00000005
22	0.00000001	22	0.00000002
23	0.00000001	23	0.00000001
24	0.00000000	24	0.00000000
25	0.00000000	25	0.00000000

For a utilization level of 50%

Probability of N units		Probability of K or more units	
N	P(N)	K	P(N>K)
0	0.49999994	0	1.00000000
1	0.25000000	1	0.50000006
2	0.12500001	2	0.25000006
3	0.06250001	3	0.12500004
4	0.03125001	4	0.06250003
5	0.01562501	5	0.03125002
6	0.00781250	6	0.01562501
7	0.00390625	7	0.00781251
8	0.00195313	8	0.00390625
9	0.00097656	9	0.00195313
10	0.00048828	10	0.00097656
11	0.00024414	11	0.00048828
12	0.00012207	12	0.00024414
13	0.00006104	13	0.00012207
14	0.00003052	14	0.00006104
15	0.00001526	15	0.00003052
16	0.00000763	16	0.00001526
17	0.00000381	17	0.00000763
18	0.00000191	18	0.00000381
19	0.00000095	19	0.00000191
20	0.00000048	20	0.00000095
21	0.00000024	21	0.00000048
22	0.00000012	22	0.00000024
23	0.00000006	23	0.00000012
24	0.00000003	24	0.00000006
25	0.00000001	25	0.00000003

For a utilization level of 55%

Probability of N units		Probability of K or more units	
N	P(N)	K	P(N>K)
0	0.44999993	0	1.00000000
1	0.24749999	1	0.55000007
2	0.13612501	2	0.30250007
3	0.07486877	3	0.16637507
4	0.04117783	4	0.09150629
5	0.02264781	5	0.05032847
6	0.01245630	6	0.02768066
7	0.00685096	7	0.01522437
8	0.00376803	8	0.00837340
9	0.00207242	9	0.00460537
10	0.00113983	10	0.00253296
11	0.00062691	11	0.00139313
12	0.00034480	12	0.00076622
13	0.00018964	13	0.00042142
14	0.00010430	14	0.00023178
15	0.00005737	15	0.00012748
16	0.00003155	16	0.00007011
17	0.00001735	17	0.00003856
18	0.00000954	18	0.00002121
19	0.00000525	19	0.00001167
20	0.00000289	20	0.00000642
21	0.00000159	21	0.00000353
22	0.00000087	22	0.00000194
23	0.00000048	23	0.00000107
24	0.00000026	24	0.00000059
25	0.00000015	25	0.00000032

For a utilization level of 60%

Probability of N units			Probability of K or more units		
N	P(N)		K	P(N>K)	
0	0.39999992		0	1.00000000	
1	0.23999998		1	0.60000008	
2	0.14400001		2	0.36000010	
3	0.08640002		3	0.21600010	
4	0.05184002		4	0.12960008	
5	0.03110402		5	0.07776006	
6	0.01866241		6	0.04665604	
7	0.01119745		7	0.02799363	
8	0.00671847		8	0.01679618	
9	0.00403108		9	0.01007771	
10	0.00241865		10	0.00604663	
11	0.00145119		11	0.00362798	
12	0.00087071		12	0.00217679	
13	0.00052243		13	0.00130607	
14	0.00031346		14	0.00078364	
15	0.00018807		15	0.00047019	
16	0.00011284		16	0.00028211	
17	0.00006771		17	0.00016927	
18	0.00004062		18	0.00010156	
19	0.00002437		19	0.00006094	
20	0.00001462		20	0.00003656	
21	0.00000877		21	0.00002194	
22	0.00000526		22	0.00001316	
23	0.00000316		23	0.00000790	
24	0.00000190		24	0.00000474	
25	0.00000114		25	0.00000284	

For a utilization level of 65%

Probability of N units			Probability of K or more units		
N	P(N)		K	P(N>K)	
0	0.34999990		0	1.00000000	
1	0.22749998		1	0.65000010	
2	0.14787500		2	0.42250013	
3	0.09611876		3	0.27462512	
4	0.06247721		4	0.17850636	
5	0.04061019		5	0.11602915	
6	0.02639663		6	0.07541896	
7	0.01715781		7	0.04902233	
8	0.01115258		8	0.03186452	
9	0.00724918		9	0.02071194	
10	0.00471197		10	0.01346276	
11	0.00306278		11	0.00875080	
12	0.00199081		12	0.00568802	
13	0.00129402		13	0.00369721	
14	0.00084112		14	0.00240319	
15	0.00054673		15	0.00156207	
16	0.00035537		16	0.00101535	
17	0.00023099		17	0.00065998	
18	0.00015014		18	0.00042898	
19	0.00009759		19	0.00027884	
20	0.00006344		20	0.00018125	
21	0.00004123		21	0.00011781	
22	0.00002680		22	0.00007658	
23	0.00001742		23	0.00004977	
24	0.00001132		24	0.00003235	
25	0.00000736		25	0.00002103	

For a utilization level of 70%			
Probability of N units		Probability of K or more units	
N	$P(N)$	K	$P(N>K)$
0	0.29999989	0	1.00000000
1	0.20999996	1	0.70000011
2	0.14700000	2	0.49000016
3	0.10290001	3	0.34300014
4	0.07203002	4	0.24010015
5	0.05042102	5	0.16807012
6	0.03529472	6	0.11764911
7	0.02470631	7	0.08235439
8	0.01729442	8	0.05764808
9	0.01210609	9	0.04035366
10	0.00847427	10	0.02824757
11	0.00593199	11	0.01977330
12	0.00415239	12	0.01384131
13	0.00290667	13	0.00968892
14	0.00203467	14	0.00678225
15	0.00142427	15	0.00474757
16	0.00099699	16	0.00332330
17	0.00069789	17	0.00232631
18	0.00048853	18	0.00162842
19	0.00034197	19	0.00113989
20	0.00023938	20	0.00079793
21	0.00016756	21	0.00055855
22	0.00011729	22	0.00039098
23	0.00008211	23	0.00027369
24	0.00005747	24	0.00019158
25	0.00004023	25	0.00013411

For a utilization level of 75%			
Probability of N units		Probability of K or more units	
N	$P(N)$	K	$P(N>K)$
0	0.24999988	0	1.00000000
1	0.18749994	1	0.75000012
2	0.14062497	2	0.56250018
3	0.10546875	3	0.42187521
4	0.07910158	4	0.31640646
5	0.05932619	5	0.23730488
6	0.04449465	6	0.17797868
7	0.03337099	7	0.13348404
8	0.02502825	8	0.10011304
9	0.01877119	9	0.07508479
10	0.01407839	10	0.05631360
11	0.01055880	11	0.04223521
12	0.00791910	12	0.03167641
13	0.00593933	13	0.02375731
14	0.00445449	14	0.01781799
15	0.00334087	15	0.01336349
16	0.00250565	16	0.01002262
17	0.00187924	17	0.00751697
18	0.00140943	18	0.00563773
19	0.00105707	19	0.00422830
20	0.00079281	20	0.00317122
21	0.00059460	21	0.00237842
22	0.00044595	22	0.00178381
23	0.00033446	23	0.00133786
24	0.00025085	24	0.00100340
25	0.00018814	25	0.00075255

For a utilization level of 80%			
Probability of N units		Probability of K or more units	
N	$P(N)$	K	$P(N>K)$
0	0.19999987	0	1.00000000
1	0.15999992	1	0.80000013
2	0.12799996	2	0.64000022
3	0.10239998	3	0.51200026
4	0.08192000	4	0.40960026
5	0.06553601	5	0.32768026
6	0.05242882	6	0.26214427
7	0.04194306	7	0.20971544
8	0.03355445	8	0.16777238
9	0.02684357	9	0.13421793
10	0.02147486	10	0.10737436
11	0.01717989	11	0.08589950
12	0.01374391	12	0.06871961
13	0.01099513	13	0.05497570
14	0.00879611	14	0.04398056
15	0.00703689	15	0.03518446
16	0.00562951	16	0.02814757
17	0.00450361	17	0.02251806
18	0.00360289	18	0.01801445
19	0.00288231	19	0.01441156
20	0.00230585	20	0.01152925
21	0.00184468	21	0.00922340
22	0.00147574	22	0.00737872
23	0.00118060	23	0.00590298
24	0.00094448	24	0.00472239
25	0.00075558	25	0.00377791

For a utilization level of 85%			
Probability of N units		Probability of K or more units	
N	$P(N)$	K	$P(N>K)$
0	0.14999986	0	1.00000000
1	0.12749989	1	0.85000014
2	0.10837493	2	0.72250026
3	0.09211871	3	0.61412531
4	0.07830092	4	0.52200663
5	0.06655579	5	0.44370568
6	0.05657243	6	0.37714991
7	0.04808657	7	0.32057747
8	0.04087359	8	0.27249089
9	0.03474256	9	0.23161730
10	0.02953118	10	0.19687474
11	0.02510151	11	0.16734356
12	0.02133629	12	0.14224204
13	0.01813585	13	0.12090576
14	0.01541547	14	0.10276991
15	0.01310315	15	0.08735444
16	0.01113768	16	0.07425129
17	0.00946703	17	0.06311361
18	0.00804698	18	0.05364657
19	0.00683993	19	0.04559959
20	0.00581394	20	0.03875966
21	0.00494185	21	0.03294572
22	0.00420058	22	0.02800386
23	0.00357049	23	0.02380329
24	0.00303492	24	0.02023280
25	0.00257968	25	0.01719788

For a utilization level of 90%

Probability of N units		Probability of K or more units	
N	P(N)	K	P(N>K)
0	0.09999985	0	1.00000000
1	0.08999988	1	0.90000015
2	0.08099990	2	0.81000030
3	0.07289992	3	0.72900039
4	0.06560995	4	0.65610045
5	0.05904896	5	0.59049052
6	0.05314407	6	0.53144157
7	0.04782967	7	0.47829747
8	0.04304671	8	0.43046781
9	0.03874205	9	0.38742110
10	0.03486785	10	0.34867904
11	0.03138107	11	0.31381118
12	0.02824297	12	0.28243011
13	0.02541868	13	0.25418717
14	0.02287681	14	0.22876848
15	0.02058913	15	0.20589167
16	0.01853022	16	0.18530253
17	0.01667720	17	0.16677231
18	0.01500949	18	0.15009511
19	0.01350854	19	0.13508561
20	0.01215769	20	0.12157708
21	0.01094192	21	0.10941938
22	0.00984773	22	0.09847746
23	0.00886296	23	0.08862973
24	0.00797667	24	0.07976677
25	0.00717900	25	0.07179011

For a utilization level of 95%

Probability of N units		Probability of K or more units	
N	P(N)	K	P(N>K)
0	0.04999983	0	1.00000000
1	0.04749985	1	0.95000017
2	0.04512487	2	0.90250033
3	0.04286863	3	0.85737544
4	0.04072521	4	0.81450683
5	0.03868895	5	0.77378160
6	0.03675451	6	0.73509264
7	0.03491679	7	0.69833815
8	0.03317096	8	0.66342139
9	0.03151242	9	0.63025039
10	0.02993680	10	0.59873801
11	0.02843997	11	0.56880116
12	0.02701797	12	0.54036123
13	0.02566708	13	0.51334327
14	0.02438373	14	0.48767617
15	0.02316455	15	0.46329245
16	0.02200632	16	0.44012791
17	0.02090601	17	0.41812158
18	0.01986071	18	0.39721557
19	0.01886768	19	0.37735486
20	0.01792430	20	0.35848719
21	0.01702809	21	0.34056288
22	0.01617669	22	0.32353479
23	0.01536785	23	0.30735812
24	0.01459946	24	0.29199025
25	0.01386949	25	0.27739078

APPENDIX B

4- AND 16-MBPS TOKEN-RING NETWORK PERFORMANCE BASED UPON THE NETWORK OPERATING RATE, NUMBER OF NETWORK STATIONS, FRAME LENGTH, AND TOTAL CABLE LENGTH

Frame rate of 4-Mbps Token-Ring network based upon the network operating rate, number of stations, frame length and total cable length

Number of stations	Avg frame length	Cable length ×000 feet	Frame rate in fps	Number of stations	Avg frame length	Cable length ×000 feet	Frame rate in fps
20	512	2	914	10	64	2	5301
20	512	4	911	10	64	4	5210
20	512	6	909	10	64	6	5123
20	512	8	906	10	64	8	5038
20	512	10	903	10	64	10	4956
20	1024	2	472	10	128	2	3158
20	1024	4	471	10	128	4	3126
20	1024	6	471	10	128	6	3094
20	1024	8	470	10	128	8	3063
20	1024	10	469	10	128	10	3032
20	2048	2	240	10	256	2	1746
20	2048	4	240	10	256	4	1736
20	2048	6	240	10	256	6	1726
20	2048	8	239	10	256	8	1717
20	2048	10	239	10	256	10	1707
20	4096	2	121	10	512	2	922
20	4096	4	121	10	512	4	919
20	4096	6	121	10	512	6	916
20	4096	8	121	10	512	8	914
20	4096	10	121	10	512	10	911
30	64	2	4821	10	1024	2	474
30	64	4	4746	10	1024	4	473
30	64	6	4674	10	1024	6	473
30	64	8	4603	10	1024	8	472
30	64	10	4535	10	1024	10	471
30	128	2	2981	10	2048	2	241
30	128	4	2953	10	2048	4	240
30	128	6	2924	10	2048	6	240
30	128	8	2896	10	2048	8	240
30	128	10	2869	10	2048	10	240
30	256	2	1691	10	4096	2	121
30	256	4	1682	10	4096	4	121
30	256	6	1672	10	4096	6	121
30	256	8	1663	10	4096	8	121
30	256	10	1654	10	4096	10	121
30	512	2	906	20	64	2	5050
30	512	4	904	20	64	4	4967
30	512	6	901	20	64	6	4888
30	512	8	898	20	64	8	4811
30	512	10	896	20	64	10	4736
30	1024	2	470	20	128	2	3067
30	1024	4	469	20	128	4	3037
30	1024	6	469	20	128	6	3007
30	1024	8	468	20	128	8	2977
30	1024	10	467	20	128	10	2949
30	2048	2	239	20	256	2	1718
30	2048	4	239	20	256	4	1708
30	2048	6	239	20	256	6	1699
30	2048	8	239	20	256	8	1690
30	2048	10	239	20	256	10	1680

Number of stations	Avg frame length	Cable length ×000 feet	Frame rate in fps	Number of stations	Avg frame length	Cable length ×000 feet	Frame rate in fps
30	4096	2	121	50	256	2	1639
30	4096	4	121	50	256	4	1630
30	4096	6	121	50	256	6	1621
30	4096	8	121	50	256	8	1613
30	4096	10	121	50	256	10	1604
40	64	2	4613	50	512	2	891
40	64	4	4544	50	512	4	889
40	64	6	4477	50	512	6	886
40	64	8	4413	50	512	8	883
40	64	10	4350	50	512	10	881
40	128	2	2900	50	1024	2	466
40	128	4	2873	50	1024	4	465
40	128	6	2846	50	1024	6	465
40	128	8	2820	50	1024	8	464
40	128	10	2794	50	1024	10	463
40	256	2	1665	50	2048	2	238
40	256	4	1655	50	2048	4	238
40	256	6	1647	50	2048	6	238
40	256	8	1638	50	2048	8	238
40	256	10	1629	50	2048	10	238
40	512	2	899	50	4096	2	121
40	512	4	896	50	4096	4	121
40	512	6	893	50	4096	6	121
40	512	8	891	50	4096	8	120
40	512	10	888	50	4096	10	120
40	1024	2	468	60	64	2	4246
40	1024	4	467	60	64	4	4187
40	1024	6	467	60	64	6	4131
40	1024	8	466	60	64	8	4075
40	1024	10	465	60	64	10	4022
40	2048	2	239	60	128	2	2751
40	2048	4	239	60	128	4	2726
40	2048	6	239	60	128	6	2702
40	2048	8	238	60	128	8	2678
40	2048	10	238	60	128	10	2655
40	4096	2	121	60	256	2	1614
40	4096	4	121	60	256	4	1606
40	4096	6	121	60	256	6	1597
40	4096	8	121	60	256	8	1589
40	4096	10	121	60	256	10	1581
50	64	2	4422	60	512	2	884
50	64	4	4359	60	512	4	881
50	64	6	4297	60	512	6	879
50	64	8	4237	60	512	8	876
50	64	10	4179	60	512	10	874
50	128	2	2824	60	1024	2	464
50	128	4	2798	60	1024	4	463
50	128	6	2772	60	1024	6	463
50	128	8	2747	60	1024	8	462
50	128	10	2723	60	1024	10	461

Number of stations	Avg frame length	Cable length ×000 feet	Frame rate in fps	Number of stations	Avg frame length	Cable length ×000 feet	Frame rate in fps
60	2048	2	238	80	128	2	2616
60	2048	4	238	80	128	4	2594
60	2048	6	238	80	128	6	2572
60	2048	8	237	80	128	8	2550
60	2048	10	237	80	128	10	2529
60	4096	2	120	80	256	2	1567
60	4096	4	120	80	256	4	1559
60	4096	6	120	80	256	6	1551
60	4096	8	120	80	256	8	1543
60	4096	10	120	80	256	10	1535
70	64	2	4083	80	512	2	869
70	64	4	4029	80	512	4	867
70	64	6	3977	80	512	6	864
70	64	8	3925	80	512	8	862
70	64	10	3876	80	512	10	860
70	128	2	2682	80	1024	2	460
70	128	4	2658	80	1024	4	459
70	128	6	2635	80	1024	6	459
70	128	8	2613	80	1024	8	458
70	128	10	2591	80	1024	10	457
70	256	2	1590	80	2048	2	237
70	256	4	1582	80	2048	4	237
70	256	6	1574	80	2048	6	236
70	256	8	1566	80	2048	8	236
70	256	10	1558	80	2048	10	236
70	512	2	876	80	4096	2	120
70	512	4	874	80	4096	4	120
70	512	6	871	80	4096	6	120
70	512	8	869	80	4096	8	120
70	512	10	867	80	4096	10	120
70	1024	2	462	90	64	2	3793
70	1024	4	461	90	64	4	3746
70	1024	6	461	90	64	6	3701
70	1024	8	460	90	64	8	3656
70	1024	10	459	90	64	10	3613
70	2048	2	237	90	128	2	2553
70	2048	4	237	90	128	4	2532
70	2048	6	237	90	128	6	2511
70	2048	8	237	90	128	8	2491
70	2048	10	237	90	128	10	2471
70	4096	2	120	90	256	2	1544
70	4096	4	120	90	256	4	1536
70	4096	6	120	90	256	6	1529
70	4096	8	120	90	256	8	1521
70	4096	10	120	90	256	10	1513
80	64	2	3933	90	512	2	862
80	64	4	3883	90	512	4	860
80	64	6	3834	90	512	6	857
80	64	8	3786	90	512	8	855
80	64	10	3740	90	512	10	853

Number of stations	Avg frame length	Cable length ×000 feet	Frame rate in fps	Number of stations	Avg frame length	Cable length ×000 feet	Frame rate in fps
90	1024	2	458	110	64	2	3541
90	1024	4	457	110	64	4	3500
90	1024	6	457	110	64	6	3461
90	1024	8	456	110	64	8	3422
90	1024	10	455	110	64	10	3384
90	2048	2	236	110	128	2	2437
90	2048	4	236	110	128	4	2417
90	2048	6	236	110	128	6	2398
90	2048	8	236	110	128	8	2380
90	2048	10	236	110	128	10	2361
90	4096	2	120	110	256	2	1501
90	4096	4	120	110	256	4	1493
90	4096	6	120	110	256	6	1486
90	4096	8	120	110	256	8	1479
90	4096	10	120	110	256	10	1472
100	64	2	3663	110	512	2	849
100	64	4	3619	110	512	4	846
100	64	6	3577	110	512	6	844
100	64	8	3535	110	512	8	842
100	64	10	3495	110	512	10	839
100	128	2	2494	110	1024	2	454
100	128	4	2473	110	1024	4	453
100	128	6	2453	110	1024	6	453
100	128	8	2434	110	1024	8	452
100	128	10	2415	110	1024	10	451
100	256	2	1522	110	2048	2	235
100	256	4	1514	110	2048	4	235
100	256	6	1507	110	2048	6	235
100	256	8	1500	110	2048	8	235
100	256	10	1492	110	2048	10	235
100	512	2	855	110	4096	2	120
100	512	4	853	110	4096	4	120
100	512	6	851	110	4096	6	120
100	512	8	848	110	4096	8	120
100	512	10	846	110	4096	10	120
100	1024	2	456	120	64	2	3427
100	1024	4	455	120	64	4	3389
100	1024	6	455	120	64	6	3352
100	1024	8	454	120	64	8	3315
100	1024	10	453	120	64	10	3280
100	2048	2	236	120	128	2	2382
100	2048	4	236	120	128	4	2364
100	2048	6	235	120	128	6	2346
100	2048	8	235	120	128	8	2328
100	2048	10	235	120	128	10	2310
100	4096	2	120	120	256	2	1480
100	4096	4	120	120	256	4	1473
100	4096	6	120	120	256	6	1466
100	4096	8	120	120	256	8	1459
100	4096	10	120	120	256	10	1452

Number of stations	Avg frame length	Cable length ×000 feet	Frame rate in fps	Number of stations	Avg frame length	Cable length ×000 feet	Frame rate in fps
120	512	2	842	130	4096	2	120
120	512	4	840	130	4096	4	119
120	512	6	837	130	4096	6	119
120	512	8	835	130	4096	8	119
120	512	10	833	130	4096	10	119
120	1024	2	452	140	64	2	3220
120	1024	4	451	140	64	4	3187
120	1024	6	451	140	64	6	3154
120	1024	8	450	140	64	8	3121
120	1024	10	449	140	64	10	3090
120	2048	2	235	140	128	2	2280
120	2048	4	235	140	128	4	2263
120	2048	6	234	140	128	6	2247
120	2048	8	234	140	128	8	2230
120	2048	10	234	140	128	10	2214
120	4096	2	120	140	256	2	1440
120	4096	4	120	140	256	4	1433
120	4096	6	120	140	256	6	1426
120	4096	8	120	140	256	8	1420
120	4096	10	119	140	256	10	1413
130	64	2	3321	140	512	2	829
130	64	4	3285	140	512	4	827
130	64	6	3250	140	512	6	824
130	64	8	3215	140	512	8	822
130	64	10	3182	140	512	10	820
130	128	2	2330	140	1024	2	448
130	128	4	2312	140	1024	4	448
130	128	6	2295	140	1024	6	447
130	128	8	2278	140	1024	8	446
130	128	10	2261	140	1024	10	446
130	256	2	1460	140	2048	2	234
130	256	4	1453	140	2048	4	234
130	256	6	1446	140	2048	6	233
130	256	8	1439	140	2048	8	233
130	256	10	1432	140	2048	10	233
130	512	2	835	140	4096	2	119
130	512	4	833	140	4096	4	119
130	512	6	831	140	4096	6	119
130	512	8	829	140	4096	8	119
130	512	10	826	140	4096	10	119
130	1024	2	450	150	64	2	3126
130	1024	4	450	150	64	4	3094
130	1024	6	449	150	64	6	3063
130	1024	8	448	150	64	8	3033
130	1024	10	448	150	64	10	3003
130	2048	2	234	150	128	2	2233
130	2048	4	234	150	128	4	2216
130	2048	6	234	150	128	6	2200
130	2048	8	234	150	128	8	2185
130	2048	10	234	150	128	10	2169

Number of stations	Avg frame length	Cable length ×000 feet	Frame rate in fps	Number of stations	Avg frame length	Cable length ×000 feet	Frame rate in fps
150	256	2	1421	160	2048	2	233
150	256	4	1414	160	2048	4	233
150	256	6	1408	160	2048	6	232
150	256	8	1401	160	2048	8	232
150	256	10	1395	160	2048	10	232
150	512	2	822	160	4096	2	119
150	512	4	820	160	4096	4	119
150	512	6	818	160	4096	6	119
150	512	8	816	160	4096	8	119
150	512	10	814	160	4096	10	119
150	1024	2	446	170	64	2	2953
150	1024	4	446	170	64	4	2925
150	1024	6	445	170	64	6	2897
150	1024	8	444	170	64	8	2869
150	1024	10	444	170	64	10	2843
150	2048	2	233	170	128	2	2143
150	2048	4	233	170	128	4	2128
150	2048	6	233	170	128	6	2113
150	2048	8	233	170	128	8	2099
150	2048	10	233	170	128	10	2084
150	4096	2	119	170	256	2	1384
150	4096	4	119	170	256	4	1378
150	4096	6	119	170	256	6	1371
150	4096	8	119	170	256	8	1365
150	4096	10	119	170	256	10	1359
160	64	2	3037	170	512	2	810
160	64	4	3007	170	512	4	808
160	64	6	2978	170	512	6	806
160	64	8	2949	170	512	8	804
160	64	10	2921	170	512	10	801
160	128	2	2187	170	1024	2	443
160	128	4	2171	170	1024	4	442
160	128	6	2156	170	1024	6	441
160	128	8	2141	170	1024	8	441
160	128	10	2126	170	1024	10	440
160	256	2	1402	170	2048	2	232
160	256	4	1396	170	2048	4	232
160	256	6	1389	170	2048	6	232
160	256	8	1383	170	2048	8	232
160	256	10	1377	170	2048	10	231
160	512	2	816	170	4096	2	119
160	512	4	814	170	4096	4	119
160	512	6	812	170	4096	6	119
160	512	8	810	170	4096	8	119
160	512	10	807	170	4096	10	119
160	1024	2	445	180	64	2	2873
160	1024	4	444	180	64	4	2846
160	1024	6	443	180	64	6	2820
160	1024	8	443	180	64	8	2794
160	1024	10	442	180	64	10	2769

Number of stations	Avg frame length	Cable length ×000 feet	Frame rate in fps	Number of stations	Avg frame length	Cable length ×000 feet	Frame rate in fps
180	128	2	2101	190	1024	2	439
180	128	4	2086	190	1024	4	438
180	128	6	2072	190	1024	6	438
180	128	8	2058	190	1024	8	437
180	128	10	2044	190	1024	10	437
180	256	2	1366	190	2048	2	231
180	256	4	1360	190	2048	4	231
180	256	6	1354	190	2048	6	231
180	256	8	1348	190	2048	8	231
180	256	10	1342	190	2048	10	230
180	512	2	804	190	4096	2	119
180	512	4	802	190	4096	4	119
180	512	6	800	190	4096	6	119
180	512	8	798	190	4096	8	119
180	512	10	795	190	4096	10	119
180	1024	2	441	200	64	2	2726
180	1024	4	440	200	64	4	2702
180	1024	6	440	200	64	6	2679
180	1024	8	439	200	64	8	2655
180	1024	10	438	200	64	10	2632
180	2048	2	232	200	128	2	2021
180	2048	4	232	200	128	4	2008
180	2048	6	231	200	128	6	1995
180	2048	8	231	200	128	8	1982
180	2048	10	231	200	128	10	1969
180	4096	2	119	200	256	2	1332
180	4096	4	119	200	256	4	1326
180	4096	6	119	200	256	6	1320
180	4096	8	119	200	256	8	1315
180	4096	10	119	200	256	10	1309
190	64	2	2798	200	512	2	792
190	64	4	2773	200	512	4	790
190	64	6	2748	200	512	6	788
190	64	8	2723	200	512	8	786
190	64	10	2699	200	512	10	784
190	128	2	2060	200	1024	2	437
190	128	4	2046	200	1024	4	437
190	128	6	2033	200	1024	6	436
190	128	8	2019	200	1024	8	435
190	128	10	2006	200	1024	10	435
190	256	2	1349	200	2048	2	231
190	256	4	1343	200	2048	4	231
190	256	6	1337	200	2048	6	230
190	256	8	1331	200	2048	8	230
190	256	10	1325	200	2048	10	230
190	512	2	798	200	4096	2	119
190	512	4	796	200	4096	4	119
190	512	6	794	200	4096	6	119
190	512	8	792	200	4096	8	118
190	512	10	790	200	4096	10	118

Number of stations	Avg frame length	Cable length ×000 feet	Frame rate in fps	Number of stations	Avg frame length	Cable length ×000 feet	Frame rate in fps
210	64	2	2658	220	512	2	780
210	64	4	2635	220	512	4	778
210	64	6	2613	220	512	6	776
210	64	8	2591	220	512	8	774
210	64	10	2569	220	512	10	772
210	128	2	1984	220	1024	2	434
210	128	4	1971	220	1024	4	433
210	128	6	1958	220	1024	6	433
210	128	8	1946	220	1024	8	432
210	128	10	1933	220	1024	10	431
210	256	2	1316	220	2048	2	230
210	256	4	1310	220	2048	4	230
210	256	6	1304	220	2048	6	229
210	256	8	1299	220	2048	8	229
210	256	10	1293	220	2048	10	229
210	512	2	786	220	4096	2	118
210	512	4	784	220	4096	4	118
210	512	6	782	220	4096	6	118
210	512	8	780	220	4096	8	118
210	512	10	778	220	4096	10	118
210	1024	2	436	230	64	2	2532
210	1024	4	435	230	64	4	2511
210	1024	6	434	230	64	6	2491
210	1024	8	434	230	64	8	2471
210	1024	10	433	230	64	10	2451
210	2048	2	230	230	128	2	1912
210	2048	4	230	230	128	4	1900
210	2048	6	230	230	128	6	1889
210	2048	8	230	230	128	8	1877
210	2048	10	230	230	128	10	1866
210	4096	2	118	230	256	2	1284
210	4096	4	118	230	256	4	1278
210	4096	6	118	230	256	6	1273
210	4096	8	118	230	256	8	1268
210	4096	10	118	230	256	10	1263
220	64	2	2594	230	512	2	775
220	64	4	2572	230	512	4	773
220	64	6	2550	230	512	6	771
220	64	8	2529	230	512	8	769
220	64	10	2508	230	512	10	767
220	128	2	1947	230	1024	2	432
220	128	4	1935	230	1024	4	431
220	128	6	1923	230	1024	6	431
220	128	8	1911	230	1024	8	430
220	128	10	1899	230	1024	10	430
220	256	2	1299	230	2048	2	229
220	256	4	1294	230	2048	4	229
220	256	6	1289	230	2048	6	229
220	256	8	1283	230	2048	8	229
220	256	10	1278	230	2048	10	229

Number of stations	Avg frame length	Cable length ×000 feet	Frame rate in fps	Number of stations	Avg frame length	Cable length ×000 feet	Frame rate in fps
230	4096	2	118	250	512	2	764
230	4096	4	118	250	512	4	762
230	4096	6	118	250	512	6	760
230	4096	8	118	250	512	8	758
230	4096	10	118	250	512	10	756
240	64	2	2474	250	1024	2	429
240	64	4	2454	250	1024	4	428
240	64	6	2434	250	1024	6	427
240	64	8	2415	250	1024	8	427
240	64	10	2396	250	1024	10	426
240	128	2	1879	250	2048	2	228
240	128	4	1867	250	2048	4	228
240	128	6	1856	250	2048	6	228
240	128	8	1845	250	2048	8	228
240	128	10	1834	250	2048	10	228
240	256	2	1269	250	4096	2	118
240	256	4	1263	250	4096	4	118
240	256	6	1258	250	4096	6	118
240	256	8	1253	250	4096	8	118
240	256	10	1248	250	4096	10	118
240	512	2	769	260	64	2	2364
240	512	4	767	260	64	4	2346
240	512	6	765	260	64	6	2328
240	512	8	763	260	64	8	2310
240	512	10	761	260	64	10	2293
240	1024	2	430	260	128	2	1815
240	1024	4	430	260	128	4	1804
240	1024	6	429	260	128	6	1793
240	1024	8	428	260	128	8	1783
240	1024	10	428	260	128	10	1773
240	2048	2	229	260	256	2	1239
240	2048	4	229	260	256	4	1234
240	2048	6	228	260	256	6	1229
240	2048	8	228	260	256	8	1224
240	2048	10	228	260	256	10	1219
240	4096	2	118	260	512	2	758
240	4096	4	118	260	512	4	756
240	4096	6	118	260	512	6	754
240	4096	8	118	260	512	8	753
240	4096	10	118	260	512	10	751
250	64	2	2417	260	1024	2	427
250	64	4	2398	260	1024	4	426
250	64	6	2380	260	1024	6	426
250	64	8	2361	260	1024	8	425
250	64	10	2343	260	1024	10	424
250	128	2	1846	260	2048	2	228
250	128	4	1835	260	2048	4	228
250	128	6	1824	260	2048	6	227
250	128	8	1813	260	2048	8	227
250	128	10	1803	260	2048	10	227
250	256	2	1254	260	4096	2	118
250	256	4	1249	260	4096	4	118
250	256	6	1243	260	4096	6	118
250	256	8	1238	260	4096	8	118
250	256	10	1233	260	4096	10	118

Frame rate of 16-Mbps Token-Ring network based upon the network operating rate, number of stations, frame length and total cable length

Number of stations	Avg frame length	Cable length ×000 feet	Frame rate in fps	Number of stations	Avg frame length	Cable length ×000 feet	Frame rate in fps
10	64	2	20152	20	512	2	3624
10	64	4	18902	20	512	4	3581
10	64	6	17799	20	512	6	3539
10	64	8	16817	20	512	8	3499
10	64	10	15938	20	512	10	3459
10	128	2	12251	20	1024	2	1880
10	128	4	11778	20	1024	4	1868
10	128	6	11340	20	1024	6	1857
10	128	8	10933	20	1024	8	1846
10	128	10	10555	20	1024	10	1835
10	256	2	6867	20	2048	2	958
10	256	4	6716	20	2048	4	955
10	256	6	6571	20	2048	6	952
10	256	8	6432	20	2048	8	949
10	256	10	6299	20	2048	10	946
10	512	2	3655	20	4096	2	484
10	512	4	3611	20	4096	4	483
10	512	6	3569	20	4096	6	482
10	512	8	3528	20	4096	8	481
10	512	10	3487	20	4096	10	481
10	1024	2	1888	30	64	2	18412
10	1024	4	1877	30	64	4	17364
10	1024	6	1865	30	64	6	16428
10	1024	8	1854	30	64	8	15588
10	1024	10	1842	30	64	10	14830
10	2048	2	960	30	128	2	11586
10	2048	4	957	30	128	4	11162
10	2048	6	954	30	128	6	10768
10	2048	8	951	30	128	8	10400
10	2048	10	948	30	128	10	10057
10	4096	2	484	30	256	2	6653
10	4096	4	483	30	256	4	6511
10	4096	6	483	30	256	6	6375
10	4096	8	482	30	256	8	6244
10	4096	10	481	30	256	10	6119
20	64	2	19243	30	512	2	3593
20	64	4	18100	30	512	4	3551
20	64	6	17086	30	512	6	3510
20	64	8	16179	30	512	8	3470
20	64	10	15364	30	512	10	3431
20	128	2	11909	30	1024	2	1872
20	128	4	11462	30	1024	4	1860
20	128	6	11046	30	1024	6	1849
20	128	8	10660	30	1024	8	1838
20	128	10	10300	30	1024	10	1827
20	256	2	6758	30	2048	2	956
20	256	4	6612	30	2048	4	953
20	256	6	6471	30	2048	6	950
20	256	8	6337	30	2048	8	947
20	256	10	6208	30	2048	10	944

Number of stations	Avg frame length	Cable length ×000 feet	Frame rate in fps	Number of stations	Avg frame length	Cable length ×000 feet	Frame rate in fps
30	4096	2	483	50	256	2	6452
30	4096	4	482	50	256	4	6318
30	4096	6	481	50	256	6	6190
30	4096	8	481	50	256	8	6067
30	4096	10	480	50	256	10	5948
40	64	2	17651	50	512	2	3534
40	64	4	16685	50	512	4	3493
40	64	6	15819	50	512	6	3454
40	64	8	15039	50	512	8	3415
40	64	10	14332	50	512	10	3377
40	128	2	11280	50	1024	2	1855
40	128	4	10877	50	1024	4	1844
40	128	6	10503	50	1024	6	1833
40	128	8	10153	50	1024	8	1822
40	128	10	9826	50	1024	10	1811
40	256	2	6551	50	2048	2	951
40	256	4	6413	50	2048	4	949
40	256	6	6281	50	2048	6	946
40	256	8	6154	50	2048	8	943
40	256	10	6032	50	2048	10	940
40	512	2	3563	50	4096	2	482
40	512	4	3522	50	4096	4	481
40	512	6	3482	50	4096	6	480
40	512	8	3442	50	4096	8	480
40	512	10	3404	50	4096	10	479
40	1024	2	1863	60	64	2	16302
40	1024	4	1852	60	64	4	15474
40	1024	6	1841	60	64	6	14727
40	1024	8	1830	60	64	8	14048
40	1024	10	1819	60	64	10	13430
40	2048	2	954	60	128	2	10713
40	2048	4	951	60	128	4	10350
40	2048	6	948	60	128	6	10010
40	2048	8	945	60	128	8	9692
40	2048	10	942	60	128	10	9393
40	4096	2	482	60	256	2	6356
40	4096	4	482	60	256	4	6226
40	4096	6	481	60	256	6	6101
40	4096	8	480	60	256	8	5981
40	4096	10	479	60	256	10	5866
50	64	2	16950	60	512	2	3505
50	64	4	16057	60	512	4	3465
50	64	6	15253	60	512	6	3426
50	64	8	14527	60	512	8	3388
50	64	10	13866	60	512	10	3351
50	128	2	10989	60	1024	2	1847
50	128	4	10607	60	1024	4	1836
50	128	6	10250	60	1024	6	1825
50	128	8	9917	60	1024	8	1814
50	128	10	9604	60	1024	10	1804

Number of stations	Avg frame length	Cable length ×000 feet	Frame rate in fps	Number of stations	Avg frame length	Cable length ×000 feet	Frame rate in fps
60	2048	2	949	80	128	2	10201
60	2048	4	946	80	128	4	9871
60	2048	6	943	80	128	6	9561
60	2048	8	941	80	128	8	9270
60	2048	10	938	80	128	10	8997
60	4096	2	481	80	256	2	6172
60	4096	4	481	80	256	4	6049
60	4096	6	480	80	256	6	5932
60	4096	8	479	80	256	8	5818
60	4096	10	478	80	256	10	5709
70	64	2	15702	80	512	2	3448
70	64	4	14933	80	512	4	3409
70	64	6	14236	80	512	6	3372
70	64	8	13601	80	512	8	3335
70	64	10	13020	80	512	10	3299
70	128	2	10451	80	1024	2	1831
70	128	4	10104	80	1024	4	1820
70	128	6	9780	80	1024	6	1810
70	128	8	9476	80	1024	8	1799
70	128	10	9191	80	1024	10	1788
70	256	2	6262	80	2048	2	945
70	256	4	6136	80	2048	4	942
70	256	6	6015	80	2048	6	939
70	256	8	5899	80	2048	8	936
70	256	10	5787	80	2048	10	934
70	512	2	3476	80	4096	2	480
70	512	4	3437	80	4096	4	480
70	512	6	3399	80	4096	6	479
70	512	8	3361	80	4096	8	478
70	512	10	3324	80	4096	10	477
70	1024	2	1839	90	64	2	14625
70	1024	4	1828	90	64	4	13956
70	1024	6	1817	90	64	6	13345
70	1024	8	1807	90	64	8	12785
70	1024	10	1796	90	64	10	12271
70	2048	2	947	90	128	2	9963
70	2048	4	944	90	128	4	9648
70	2048	6	941	90	128	6	9352
70	2048	8	939	90	128	8	9073
70	2048	10	936	90	128	10	8811
70	4096	2	481	90	256	2	6084
70	4096	4	480	90	256	4	5965
70	4096	6	479	90	256	6	5850
70	4096	8	479	90	256	8	5740
70	4096	10	478	90	256	10	5634
80	64	2	15145	90	512	2	3420
80	64	4	14428	90	512	4	3382
80	64	6	13776	90	512	6	3345
80	64	8	13180	90	512	8	3309
80	64	10	12634	90	512	10	3273

Number of stations	Avg frame length	Cable length ×000 feet	Frame rate in fps	Number of stations	Avg frame length	Cable length ×000 feet	Frame rate in fps
90	1024	2	1824	110	64	2	13687
90	1024	4	1813	110	64	4	13099
90	1024	6	1802	110	64	6	12559
90	1024	8	1791	110	64	8	12063
90	1024	10	1781	110	64	10	11603
90	2048	2	943	110	128	2	9518
90	2048	4	940	110	128	4	9230
90	2048	6	937	110	128	6	8959
90	2048	8	934	110	128	8	8703
90	2048	10	932	110	128	10	8462
90	4096	2	480	110	256	2	5915
90	4096	4	479	110	256	4	5802
90	4096	6	478	110	256	6	5694
90	4096	8	478	110	256	8	5590
90	4096	10	477	110	256	10	5489
100	64	2	14141	110	512	2	3366
100	64	4	13514	110	512	4	3330
100	64	6	12940	110	512	6	3294
100	64	8	12413	110	512	8	3258
100	64	10	11928	110	512	10	3224
100	128	2	9735	110	1024	2	1808
100	128	4	9434	110	1024	4	1797
100	128	6	9151	110	1024	6	1787
100	128	8	8884	110	1024	8	1777
100	128	10	8633	110	1024	10	1766
100	256	2	5998	110	2048	2	939
100	256	4	5882	110	2048	4	936
100	256	6	5771	110	2048	6	933
100	256	8	5664	110	2048	8	930
100	256	10	5561	110	2048	10	927
100	512	2	3393	110	4096	2	479
100	512	4	3356	110	4096	4	478
100	512	6	3319	110	4096	6	477
100	512	8	3283	110	4096	8	476
100	512	10	3248	110	4096	10	476
100	1024	2	1816	120	64	2	13262
100	1024	4	1805	120	64	4	12709
100	1024	6	1794	120	64	6	12200
100	1024	8	1784	120	64	8	11731
100	1024	10	1774	120	64	10	11296
100	2048	2	941	120	128	2	9311
100	2048	4	938	120	128	4	9035
100	2048	6	935	120	128	6	8775
100	2048	8	932	120	128	8	8529
100	2048	10	930	120	128	10	8297
100	4096	2	479	120	256	2	5834
100	4096	4	478	120	256	4	5725
100	4096	6	478	120	256	6	5619
100	4096	8	477	120	256	8	5517
100	4096	10	476	120	256	10	5419

Number of stations	Avg frame length	Cable length ×000 feet	Frame rate in fps	Number of stations	Avg frame length	Cable length ×000 feet	Frame rate in fps
130	4096	2	478	120	512	2	3340
130	4096	4	477	120	512	4	3304
130	4096	6	476	120	512	6	3268
130	4096	8	475	120	512	8	3234
130	4096	10	475	120	512	10	3200
140	64	2	12486	120	1024	2	1800
140	64	4	11994	120	1024	4	1790
140	64	6	11540	120	1024	6	1779
140	64	8	11119	120	1024	8	1769
140	64	10	10728	120	1024	10	1759
140	128	2	8921	120	2048	2	937
140	128	4	8668	120	2048	4	934
140	128	6	8428	120	2048	6	931
140	128	8	8201	120	2048	8	928
140	128	10	7986	120	2048	10	925
140	256	2	5679	120	4096	2	478
140	256	4	5575	120	4096	4	477
140	256	6	5475	120	4096	6	477
140	256	8	5378	120	4096	8	476
140	256	10	5285	120	4096	10	475
140	512	2	3288	130	64	2	12862
140	512	4	3253	130	64	4	12341
140	512	6	3219	130	64	6	11861
140	512	8	3185	130	64	8	11417
140	512	10	3152	130	64	10	11005
140	1024	2	1785	130	128	2	9112
140	1024	4	1775	130	128	4	8847
140	1024	6	1765	130	128	6	8598
140	1024	8	1755	130	128	8	8362
140	1024	10	1745	130	128	10	8139
140	2048	2	933	130	256	2	5755
140	2048	4	930	130	256	4	5649
140	2048	6	927	130	256	6	5546
140	2048	8	924	130	256	8	5447
140	2048	10	921	130	256	10	5351
140	4096	2	477	130	512	2	3314
140	4096	4	476	130	512	4	3278
140	4096	6	476	130	512	6	3244
140	4096	8	475	130	512	8	3209
140	4096	10	474	130	512	10	3176
150	64	2	12131	130	1024	2	1793
150	64	4	11666	130	1024	4	1782
150	64	6	11236	130	1024	6	1772
150	64	8	10837	130	1024	8	1762
150	64	10	10465	130	1024	10	1752
150	128	2	8738	130	2048	2	935
150	128	4	8495	130	2048	4	932
150	128	6	8265	130	2048	6	929
150	128	8	8047	130	2048	8	926
150	128	10	7840	130	2048	10	923

Number of stations	Avg frame length	Cable length ×000 feet	Frame rate in fps	Number of stations	Avg frame length	Cable length ×000 feet	Frame rate in fps
150	256	2	5604	160	2048	2	929
150	256	4	5503	160	2048	4	926
150	256	6	5406	160	2048	6	923
150	256	8	5311	160	2048	8	920
150	256	10	5220	160	2048	10	918
150	512	2	3263	160	4096	2	476
150	512	4	3229	160	4096	4	475
150	512	6	3195	160	4096	6	475
150	512	8	3162	160	4096	8	474
150	512	10	3129	160	4096	10	473
150	1024	2	1778	170	64	2	11478
150	1024	4	1768	170	64	4	11061
150	1024	6	1757	170	64	6	10674
150	1024	8	1747	170	64	8	10313
150	1024	10	1737	170	64	10	9976
150	2048	2	931	170	128	2	8395
150	2048	4	928	170	128	4	8170
150	2048	6	925	170	128	6	7956
150	2048	8	922	170	128	8	7754
150	2048	10	919	170	128	10	7562
150	4096	2	477	170	256	2	5461
150	4096	4	476	170	256	4	5365
150	4096	6	475	170	256	6	5272
150	4096	8	474	170	256	8	5182
150	4096	10	474	170	256	10	5096
160	64	2	11795	170	512	2	3214
160	64	4	11356	170	512	4	3181
160	64	6	10948	170	512	6	3148
160	64	8	10569	170	512	8	3116
160	64	10	10215	170	512	10	3084
160	128	2	8563	170	1024	2	1763
160	128	4	8329	170	1024	4	1753
160	128	6	8108	170	1024	6	1743
160	128	8	7898	170	1024	8	1733
160	128	10	7698	170	1024	10	1723
160	256	2	5532	170	2048	2	927
160	256	4	5433	170	2048	4	924
160	256	6	5338	170	2048	6	921
160	256	8	5246	170	2048	8	918
160	256	10	5157	170	2048	10	916
160	512	2	3239	170	4096	2	475
160	512	4	3205	170	4096	4	475
160	512	6	3171	170	4096	6	474
160	512	8	3139	170	4096	8	473
160	512	10	3107	170	4096	10	473
160	1024	2	1771	180	64	2	11177
160	1024	4	1760	180	64	4	10782
160	1024	6	1750	180	64	6	10414
160	1024	8	1740	180	64	8	10070
160	1024	10	1730	180	64	10	9748

Number of stations	Avg frame length	Cable length ×000 feet	Frame rate in fps	Number of stations	Avg frame length	Cable length ×000 feet	Frame rate in fps
180	128	2	8233	190	1024	2	1749
180	128	4	8016	190	1024	4	1739
180	128	6	7811	190	1024	6	1729
180	128	8	7616	190	1024	8	1719
180	128	10	7430	190	1024	10	1710
180	256	2	5392	190	2048	2	923
180	256	4	5298	190	2048	4	920
180	256	6	5208	190	2048	6	917
180	256	8	5120	190	2048	8	914
180	256	10	5036	190	2048	10	912
180	512	2	3190	190	4096	2	474
180	512	4	3157	190	4096	4	474
180	512	6	3125	190	4096	6	473
180	512	8	3093	190	4096	8	472
180	512	10	3062	190	4096	10	471
180	1024	2	1756	200	64	2	10621
180	1024	4	1746	200	64	4	10263
180	1024	6	1736	200	64	6	9929
180	1024	8	1726	200	64	8	9616
180	1024	10	1716	200	64	10	9322
180	2048	2	925	200	128	2	7927
180	2048	4	922	200	128	4	7726
180	2048	6	919	200	128	6	7535
180	2048	8	916	200	128	8	7353
180	2048	10	914	200	128	10	7180
180	4096	2	475	200	256	2	5259
180	4096	4	474	200	256	4	5170
180	4096	6	473	200	256	6	5083
180	4096	8	473	200	256	8	5000
180	4096	10	472	200	256	10	4919
190	64	2	10892	200	512	2	3143
190	64	4	10516	200	512	4	3111
190	64	6	10166	200	512	6	3080
190	64	8	9838	200	512	8	3049
190	64	10	9530	200	512	10	3019
190	128	2	8077	200	1024	2	1742
190	128	4	7868	200	1024	4	1732
190	128	6	7670	200	1024	6	1722
190	128	8	7482	200	1024	8	1712
190	128	10	7303	200	1024	10	1703
190	256	2	5324	200	2048	2	921
190	256	4	5233	200	2048	4	918
190	256	6	5145	200	2048	6	915
190	256	8	5059	200	2048	8	912
190	256	10	4977	200	2048	10	910
190	512	2	3166	200	4096	2	474
190	512	4	3134	200	4096	4	473
190	512	6	3102	200	4096	6	472
190	512	8	3071	200	4096	8	472
190	512	10	3040	200	4096	10	471

Number of stations	Avg frame length	Cable length ×000 feet	Frame rate in fps	Number of stations	Avg frame length	Cable length ×000 feet	Frame rate in fps
210	64	2	10363	220	512	2	3097
210	64	4	10022	220	512	4	3066
210	64	6	9703	220	512	6	3036
210	64	8	9404	220	512	8	3006
210	64	10	9123	220	512	10	2977
210	128	2	7782	220	1024	2	1728
210	128	4	7588	220	1024	4	1718
210	128	6	7404	220	1024	6	1708
210	128	8	7229	220	1024	8	1699
210	128	10	7061	220	1024	10	1689
210	256	2	5195	220	2048	2	917
210	256	4	5108	220	2048	4	914
210	256	6	5024	220	2048	6	911
210	256	8	4942	220	2048	8	909
210	256	10	4863	220	2048	10	906
210	512	2	3120	220	4096	2	473
210	512	4	3089	220	4096	4	472
210	512	6	3058	220	4096	6	471
210	512	8	3027	220	4096	8	471
210	512	10	2997	220	4096	10	470
210	1024	2	1735	230	64	2	9883
210	1024	4	1725	230	64	4	9572
210	1024	6	1715	230	64	6	9281
210	1024	8	1705	230	64	8	9007
210	1024	10	1696	230	64	10	8748
210	2048	2	919	230	128	2	7508
210	2048	4	916	230	128	4	7328
210	2048	6	913	230	128	6	7156
210	2048	8	910	230	128	8	6992
210	2048	10	908	230	128	10	6835
210	4096	2	473	230	256	2	5071
210	4096	4	473	230	256	4	4988
210	4096	6	472	230	256	6	4908
210	4096	8	471	230	256	8	4830
210	4096	10	470	230	256	10	4755
220	64	2	10117	230	512	2	3075
220	64	4	9792	230	512	4	3044
220	64	6	9487	230	512	6	3014
220	64	8	9201	230	512	8	2985
220	64	10	8932	230	512	10	2956
220	128	2	7643	230	1024	2	1721
220	128	4	7456	230	1024	4	1711
220	128	6	7278	230	1024	6	1701
220	128	8	7108	230	1024	8	1692
220	128	10	6946	230	1024	10	1683
220	256	2	5132	230	2048	2	915
220	256	4	5047	230	2048	4	912
220	256	6	4965	230	2048	6	909
220	256	8	4886	230	2048	8	907
220	256	10	4809	230	2048	10	904

Number of stations	Avg frame length	Cable length ×000 feet	Frame rate in fps	Number of stations	Avg frame length	Cable length ×000 feet	Frame rate in fps
230	4096	2	472	250	512	2	3031
230	4096	4	472	250	512	4	3002
230	4096	6	471	250	512	6	2972
230	4096	8	470	250	512	8	2944
230	4096	10	469	250	512	10	2916
240	64	2	9659	250	1024	2	1707
240	64	4	9362	250	1024	4	1697
240	64	6	9083	250	1024	6	1688
240	64	8	8821	250	1024	8	1679
240	64	10	8573	250	1024	10	1669
240	128	2	7378	250	2048	2	911
240	128	4	7204	250	2048	4	908
240	128	6	7038	250	2048	6	905
240	128	8	6879	250	2048	8	903
240	128	10	6727	250	2048	10	900
240	256	2	5012	250	4096	2	471
240	256	4	4931	250	4096	4	471
240	256	6	4852	250	4096	6	470
240	256	8	4776	250	4096	8	469
240	256	10	4703	250	4096	10	468
240	512	2	3053	260	64	2	9241
240	512	4	3023	260	64	4	8969
240	512	6	2993	260	64	6	8713
240	512	8	2964	260	64	8	8470
240	512	10	2936	260	64	10	8241
240	1024	2	1714	260	128	2	7132
240	1024	4	1704	260	128	4	6969
240	1024	6	1695	260	128	6	6813
240	1024	8	1685	260	128	8	6664
240	1024	10	1676	260	128	10	6522
240	2048	2	913	260	256	2	4897
240	2048	4	910	260	256	4	4819
240	2048	6	907	260	256	6	4744
240	2048	8	905	260	256	8	4672
240	2048	10	902	260	256	10	4601
240	4096	2	472	260	512	2	3010
240	4096	4	471	260	512	4	2981
240	4096	6	470	260	512	6	2952
240	4096	8	470	260	512	8	2923
240	4096	10	469	260	512	10	2896
250	64	2	9445	260	1024	2	1700
250	64	4	9161	260	1024	4	1691
250	64	6	8894	260	1024	6	1681
250	64	8	8642	260	1024	8	1672
250	64	10	8404	260	1024	10	1663
250	128	2	7253	260	2048	2	909
250	128	4	7084	260	2048	4	906
250	128	6	6924	260	2048	6	904
250	128	8	6770	260	2048	8	901
250	128	10	6623	260	2048	10	898
250	256	2	4954	260	4096	2	471
250	256	4	4874	260	4096	4	470
250	256	6	4798	260	4096	6	469
250	256	8	4723	260	4096	8	469
250	256	10	4651	260	4096	10	468

INDEX

Index compiled by Geoffrey C. Jones

LOCAL AREA NETWORKING

LAN PERFORMANCE
Issues and Answers

The performance of LANs depends upon A large number of variables, including the access method, the media and cable length, the bridging and the gateway methods. This text covers all these variables to enable the reader to select and design equipment for reliability and high performance.
1994   0 471 94223 5

TOKEN-RING NETWORKS
Characteristics, Operation, Construction and Management

The Token-Ring Network is an efficient and increasingly popular network for the office environment. This timely book provides the reader with a comprehensive understanding of how Token-Ring networks operate, the constraints and performance issues that affect their implementation, and how their growth and use can be managed both locally and as part of an Enterprise network. A description of FFDI is strategically located in the centre of the book. Succeeding chapters cover bridges, routers, gateways and include examples of the expansion and interconnection of Token-Ring and FDDI networks.
1993   0 471 94041 0

ETHERNET NETWORKS
Design, Implementation,
Operation and Management
1994   0 471 59717 1

PERSONAL COMPUTING

THE LAPTOP/NOTEBOOK
COMPANION
1993   0 471 55804 4 (Cloth)
**   0 471 55805 2 (Paper)**

REFERENCE

THE COMPLETE MODEM
REFERENCE
2nd Edition
1994   0 471 00852 4

DATA AND COMPUTER
COMMUNICATIONS
Terms, Definitions and
Abbreviations
1989   0 471 92066 5

THE COMPLETE PC AT AND
COMPATIBLES REFERENCE
MANUAL
1991   0 471 53315 7